BETWEEN DIRECTOR AND ACTOR

BETWEEN DIRECTOR AND ACTOR

Strategies for Effective Performance

Mandy Rees   John Staniunas

HEINEMANN
Portsmouth, NH

Heinemann
A division of Reed Elsevier Inc.
361 Hanover Street
Portsmouth, NH 03801-3912
www.heinemanndrama.com

Offices and agents throughout the world

Library of Congress Cataloging-in-Publication Data
Rees, Mandy.
    Between director and actor : strategies for effective performance / Mandy Rees, John Staniunas.
        p.   cm.
    ISBN 0-325-00432-3 (alk. paper)
    1. Theater—Production and direction.   2. Acting.   3. Note-taking.
I. Staniunas, John.   II. Title.

PN2053 .R35   2002
792'.028—dc21   2002006652

Editor: Lisa Barnett
Production service: TechBooks
Production coordinator: Elizabeth Valway
Cover design: Jenny Jensen Greenleaf
Typesetter: TechBooks
Manufacturing: Steve Bernier

Printed in the United States of America on acid-free paper
06   05   04   03   02   DA   1   2   3   4   5

Worthy the note.

—Shakespeare

Contents

Acknowledgments

The information for this book was drawn from our experiences with many directors, actors, teachers, students and colleagues, as well as from books and articles we have read and absorbed over the years. We acknowledge these sources collectively, and recognize our indebtedness to them.

We want to acknowledge the following institutions without whose support this book would not be possible: University of Kansas for a New Faculty Research Grant and Kimbell Faculty Enrichment Grant, California State University–Bakersfield for a sabbatical leave and Faculty Teaching & Learning Center Grant, and the University of Wisconsin for a Research Service Award. We also want to thank the Madison Repertory Theatre and Scott Glasser for allowing us to codirect a show together while we were writing.

We are extremely grateful to those artists whom we interviewed for this book and thank them for being so gracious with their time. We especially acknowledge the aid of Scott Ellis, who helped to arrange a number of interviews for us while he was in the middle of a technical rehearsal.

Thanks to Lisa Barnett and the entire Heinemann team for their enthusiastic support of our project. Also thanks to Karen Ettinger and the group at TechBooks.

And, in no particular order, but of equal importance to us for their valued support and efforts on our behalf as we struggled with the beginning, middle, and end of the process: Anita DuPratt, John Gronbeck-Tedesco, Elizabeth Carlin Metz, Shirley Vohs, Karen Prager, Karen Ryker, Mary Karen Dahl, Hazel Rees, Joseph and Barbara Staniunas, Sarah L. Young, Carolyn Martin, Kevin Robison, Rosalind Grigsby, Jim Riker, Helen Bryant, Ellen Anthony, Craig Baldwin, Harold W. Dixon, Richard T. Hanson, Dianne J. Winslow, Wilbur Rees, and Sarah Pia Anderson.

Introduction

Once upon a time there were some actors working with a director on a play. At the end of a run-through of the show, the director had the cast sit down in the audience for a "note" session. He proceeded to offer his thoughts and ideas on what the actors had done and on how they could improve on their performances. One actor received a note he had gotten several times before, while working on plays with other directors. Intrigued by this, he started to listen more intently not only to his own notes but also to the notes being given to the other actors. They sounded very familiar to him. As the director worked through his thoughts, the actor began to notice a pattern in thinking. The director's notes ranged from the general to the specific, from the very technical to the more subjective, but all the notes had one theme in common, namely, how to make the story of the play more clear to the audience.

This is a book about the collaboration that occurs between actor and director in the rehearsal and performance process. It is specifically about how directors communicate to actors through notes, and how actors use those notes to shape their performances, a process always used but rarely written about in the theatre. This book is meant to stimulate conversation and communication between directors and actors. The director–actor relationship is about defining ideas and fixing problems. As actors, we work with a variety of directors. As directors, we work with even more actors. Every actor has a unique way of working on a role; every director has a different way of phrasing thoughts and ideas. This book is meant as a resource for actors and directors in clarifying language. There are many practical ways to use it.

The major portion of this book includes sixty-five notes, both beginning and advanced, that a director might communicate to an actor during the rehearsal process. The notes have been broken down into categories and arranged according to topics of interest. Though it is possible to read through the entire text from cover to cover, the notes are also there to pick and choose from depending on the problem at hand.

For actors, this book can help to clarify and interpret notes given by the director. Even when under the guidance of either a director rehearsing a play or a teacher in an acting class, actors often need to work on their own. This book is here as a reference guide to help actors improve and refine their craft. Though an actor's technique may be strong in some areas, it may be weaker in others. Using the chapter headings as a guide, actors can look up and sort out any particular problems that may be occurring on a regular basis and find ways to address them.

For directors, particularly ones at the beginning of their career, whose knowledge of working with actors may be limited, this book can help with methods of coaching and communicating with actors. Experienced directors may find this book useful in furthering their understanding of an actor's process and pinpointing problems they may encounter. Directors may instinctively sense problems as they watch and listen in rehearsal but be at a loss as to how to guide the actors. Rather than saying something hastily, a quick glance at the list of notes from the appropriate chapter may lead to formulating a way of communicating a general thought on the problem into something much more specific. All the notes are common to the process of working on any play. Finding a way to rephrase an old note can often prove to be very effective. The book is also meant as a reminder, through various techniques, of how best to communicate notes to actors.

There are a variety of ways to say the same thing. Each note begins with one or more ways it might be phrased and with a brief description of "the problem" that triggered the giving of the note. For each note, we have tried to find the best possible way of describing a particular "problem" the actor may be encountering. Some notes such as "Clean up your diction" are fairly straightforward. Other notes, such as "Raise the stakes," may have a series of subnotes, such as "Upgrade the objective," "Fight harder for what you want," and "Make it more important" to help clarify the problem.

After each note, there is a detailed "explanation," and then a series of "strategies." The strategies are a means of approaching the problem usefully, practically, and positively. Directors can use these strategies to coach their actors, or actors can try them on their own. The actors can also try improvising with their own strategies to fix the problem. A special segment called "Additional Thoughts for the Director" gives specific advice for directors as they confront the note. Last, related notes of interest are listed.

In attempting to compile as broad a range of notes as possible, we had the distinct fortune and pleasure of interviewing eleven professional directors and actors currently working in regional and Broadway theatres. These directors and actors come from varying backgrounds and work in a wide range of theatrical genres and styles. We asked them questions about the rehearsal process, techniques of communication, and specifically about note giving and taking. There are quotes inserted at the end of some notes, and the final chapters include excerpts from our interviews.

Think of this book as a lighthouse in the fog. The beacon is there to guide you to the shore, help navigate you through a tricky passage to safety. There is always risk involved, but the reward is worth the effort. Finally, if you have a note that we neglected to include, send it to us. Give us a note, we will take it willingly.

BETWEEN DIRECTOR AND ACTOR

For the Director

Giving Notes

This book is designed, in part, to help directors pinpoint what is needed in a performance and to provide some useful strategies to use while coaching actors. As important as knowing *what* to say to actors, is knowing *how* to say it. An effective, personal style of giving notes takes many years to develop and can be a stumbling block for young directors. Finding the balance between explaining and inspiring, between being firm and being gentle, and between being precise and being flexible is an art form in itself. As directors gain experience and encounter more types of actors, knowing what note to give and when to give it becomes more of an instinct. But as every director would probably admit, there is always room to refine this important skill of communicating with actors.

The energy and tone of the director during notes can have a major impact on how actors feel. A friendly and confident demeanor is normally effective, though there may be times that call for either a tough disciplinary tone or a supportive and comforting one. Actors can usually detect insincerity, especially when a director is doling out compliments about how well the show is going, but the praise does not seem to be heartfelt. Conversely, directors who try to intimidate their actors, delivering their comments with no room for discussion, appear more as dictators than as collaborators. This technique is rarely effective, and the director is likely to lose the trust and creative contributions the actors can offer. If a director can inspire actors to work enthusiastically *with* rather than *for* him/her, this will produce the best results. Allowing for disagreement and discussion opens the door for actors to invest more of themselves into the production.

1

The first consideration before giving a note is whether the actor is ready to hear the information. During the initial stages of rehearsal, the director may know exactly what the actor could do to polish a characterization, but the actor still needs time to become familiar with the role and begin to connect with it. To skip to polishing notes would deprive the actor the chance to gain some confidence in what he is doing and might actually undermine the performance. It is also likely the actor may not be able to understand or process such notes yet, still being focused on more elementary elements such as memorization or the clarification of given circumstances.

The director needs to "sense" what the actor is ready to hear. Not all actors progress at the same rate. Just because you are in week three of rehearsal does not mean all actors should be receiving the same kind of notes. If an actor is struggling with a certain element of a performance, it is best to let her begin to master it or at least get some level of security before worrying about the next step. However, some actors may be ready and anxious to be pushed, and it is good to challenge them so they won't become frustrated or bored. Knowing when to give which note comes with experience. Of course the timing of notes changes based on the length of the rehearsal period and the experience level of the actors. Being familiar with particular actors or ensembles is certainly an advantage. Working with a new group of actors takes more awareness. In this situation, the director needs to take the time to adjust to each new actor's specific needs.

Try not to overwhelm an actor with notes. Even if there are many necessary details that need to be addressed, try to keep the number of notes per actor at a reasonable level. If actors hear too many notes, they will be unable to absorb them all and may think they are failing at their roles because they warrant so much "correction." Prioritize the essential notes, and work from there. If you can identify a core problem and help the actor to solve it, many other elements may naturally remedy themselves. Let actors focus on a few things at a time and feel challenged, rather than overloading their circuits.

You will find if you are patient and trust the actors, they will work on their own to solve problems, giving them the opportunity to come up with creative ideas, which may never have occurred to you. When they are able to make their own discoveries, they have a richer grasp of what they are doing. Some notes are better if they are held back for awhile and then only given if the actors are unable to make the improvements on their own.

Phrasing your notes also deserves some attention. Being clear and specific allows the actor to get right to work rather than spending time trying to decipher what you meant. Vague or uncertain comments tend to confuse actors and may cause them to wonder if you know what you want. If you are not certain about your choices (and being undecided about moments is normal), be open with the cast about your dilemma and give them one specific choice you want to try first. In this way you are still being clear about what you want the actors to work on, yet expressing it in such a way so the actors know they are still in an exploratory period of rehearsal. You keep them informed about the process rather than appearing indecisive or capricious. Another option is to be silent about a moment, until you have an idea of how to fix it.

Sometimes you may need to justify a note or explain your perspective in order for an actor to be willing to make a change. This is especially true when one choice has been rehearsed for an extended period of time, but the moment is not working and you want to try something new. Make sure the actor does not feel at fault or inadequate at carrying out the original choice. Your phrasing of the note can make the difference in what attitude the actor takes toward the moment. Reassure the actor that the effort has been worthwhile and perhaps has even illuminated a new solution. Then explain why you believe the new approach will work better.

If you find you are giving the same note over and over, vary your phrasing. Look for new words, new metaphors and images, and new examples to get your idea across. Ask for help—what are the actor's ideas? Sometimes by inviting insights and suggestions, you can quickly solve a problem that has been puzzling you for many rehearsals.

Be careful in your note giving not to place blame, accuse, or belittle actors. Even a casual remark about an ignorant choice may be interpreted as a slap in the face. Actors' egos are notoriously delicate, and it pays to be careful about how you express yourself. Make note sessions a time to inspire actors rather than to pass judgment on them. If actors feel they are on the firing line, they will most likely get defensive or even shut down and become very hard to direct.

As stress and time pressures build, some directors become harsh and abrasive in their commentaries. Stories of a director threatening actors, yelling at them, and cornering or badgering individuals unfortunately exist in the theatre. In an ideal world, a director would never be adversely affected by stress or temper. But it can and does happen. The results are typical: the director loses the ability to think clearly, and the cast becomes demoralized. Backstage whisperings begin, and the tenor of the rehearsals changes to the director versus the cast. If you notice frustration is coloring all your notes, it is probably time to take some measures that will help to relax you and allow your rational side to regain control. Though venting emotions sometimes is inevitable, efficiency and morale may be compromised.

Actors often look to the director to judge whether the show is doing well and whether their performances are in line. If notes only focus on what needs to be fixed, usually paramount in the director's mind, the cast may believe the show is in bad shape. It is important to both reinforce the positive and reassure the actors that their work is effective and appreciated. It is amazing how easy it is to neglect these simple tasks.

As actors respond to notes and make adjustments, some recognition is warranted. Actors frequently wonder if they fulfilled the director's request ("Is that what she wanted?" "I wonder how I looked.") Without feedback, it is possible for actors to think the director gave up on them and their performance was not worth a comment. To acknowledge every change an actor makes would be cumbersome and time consuming, but to remark on significant or difficult modifications is very useful to the actor.

In general, a director should be aware of how the cast is responding to notes. It is helpful to look up from the note pad and check in with the body language and expressions of the actors. This way, distress, anger, or resentment can quickly be identified and dealt with. If one actor is receiving a disproportionate number of notes, this may cause him/her to worry, especially when reassurance is not given. If you see panic in the actor's eyes, skip some of your less significant notes and save them for later. Likewise, someone who is not receiving any notes may feel neglected or bored. Try to give everyone a note, even if it is just one that says "good job" on a certain moment. Tensions between actors are important to notice; often as the director you can play a role in alleviating them. And most frequent, by being aware of how your comments are being received, you can pick up on actors who disagree, are uncomfortable, or don't understand your notes. This knowledge will save time and help you to avoid discord.

Methods of Giving Notes

There are several methods to giving notes. These methods are intended to be used when running through the play in larger sections or in its entirety, rather than at a stop-and-go stage.

The classic method is for the director to take notes on a legal pad, gather the cast together, and read the notes through. To make notes quicker to identify, it is useful to have abbreviations for each cast member and for each technical department, which the director writes at the beginning of each note. This way you are able to scan the left side of the page and find notes for a certain person without much effort. If you do not want to have a general session, each actor can "check in" with you for their individual notes. As notes are given, they are either scratched off the page if completed or circled if they need to be addressed further. You can also have an assistant director take notes by sitting next to you during the run and writing down your comments. Another method is to hold a compact tape recorder and dictate your thoughts into it. Some directors find this much less cumbersome than trying to write everything down. You either take the tape home and transcribe your notes or play the tape for your cast note by note and elaborate in between, though this can take a great deal of time.

To make note-giving sessions shorter, you can use a small message pad and write each note on an individual sheet of paper with the actor's abbreviation at the top. Then sort notes into separate piles and hand them over directly to each actor. Some notes will be for more than one person or for the entire group, which you keep in a pile for yourself. Gather the cast together and give these more general notes and then allow for questions and clarifications on individual items. This method demands a lot of fast writing so that your notes are understandable. If a note is too complicated to explain quickly, you can write the subject of the note and have the actor ask you for clarification. This method can significantly reduce the amount of time actors must sit around and listen to notes for others. Actors can benefit from hearing notes that do not directly apply to them, so you can decide which notes might offer some insights to the cast as a whole. Also remember to alert all actors involved when a major change is made, and not just the actor who is executing it.

Another option to the note session is to post notes on the callboard the next day. The advantage to this method is especially evident after long or arduous rehearsals, when the actors are able to go home immediately rather than wait around for notes. Long note sessions in this case are usually not very productive. This also gives you a little extra time to think about the notes and find the best way to phrase your ideas. Notes can either be posted separately for each individual to take off the board or written as a longer page for everyone to read. In the latter case, actors have to copy down their own notes, which can serve to reinforce them. Whether you want to have a chance to talk as a group after a run or give the cast time to rest will depend on a variety of factors that will vary from production to production.

One strategy to help actors connect more deeply with their roles is to use character names when giving notes or working in rehearsal. In this method the director addresses actors by their character's name, and likewise actors respond in the first person when referring to their character. For example, a director working on *A Streetcar Named Desire* might say to an actor, "Blanche, when you come down the stairs chasing after Stella, be sure you stay in the shadows." The actor might reply, "I stepped forward because I feel at that moment I am losing Stella, my only living link to my family." By asking an actor to respond in character, she engages more closely with the character's problems, motivations, and desires.

When just running scenes or acts, immediate feedback is effective. Notes can be detailed; usually you are still doing a lot of "tinkering" with the scene and the actors are open to changes. During run-throughs you begin to look at the overall picture and can worry about the flow of the show. Numerous notes are typical as past work is now seen in a clearer light. Remember to pay attention to the needs and attitudes of the actors at this stage and to address them accordingly. Once the technical and dress rehearsals begin, it is time to evaluate what you can reasonably expect each actor to achieve in the remaining few rehearsals. To bombard actors with too many notes at this stage will clutter their heads with details. Rather, they should be focused on pulling all the elements of their performance together. Positive notes wisely outnumber corrections and changes, unless unavoidable, such as in the case of a new play still undergoing rewrites. Even in this instance, acknowledging progress is crucial. Sometimes you may have an actor who is not able to accomplish all that you have set out. Now is the time to help the actor readjust goals and gain confidence.

Taking Notes

Receiving feedback from the director is an essential part of refining and sculpting your performance. Because you are unable to step back from your own work and see it objectively, you have to rely on the eye of the director. How your performance is coming across, how clear you are, how your work is blending with the overall picture—these things can only be evaluated by someone who is able to view a performance from the audience's perspective. Actors who have had to work on projects without a director quickly learn the benefits of good notes and are grateful for the input.

When the director gives you a note orally it is a good idea to write it down, especially if there is any chance you may forget it before the next rehearsal. If you do not understand or are confused about a note, it is important to clarify the director's message either by asking questions or by requesting elaboration. In any case, the director's ideal is to have a note understood and executed by the next rehearsal of that scene. To forget, ignore, or remain unclear about a note is to slow down the rehearsal process. By doing so, you prevent the director from helping you to advance your performance, forcing the director to give the same notes repeatedly and causing frustration for both of you.

Though the act of "receiving notes" would not at first glance appear to be very difficult, many actors have a hard time with it. Some actors fight what they are told, some become depressed because they feel criticized, and others are compelled to defend themselves. If you remind yourself of the purpose of note sessions and the benefits they provide, you are more likely to be gracious when given a note.

Avoid the need to explain why you did something every time you get a note. Some actors will try to clarify why they made a certain choice, what they were thinking about, and why they agree or disagree with the director's viewpoint. Though sometimes it may be appropriate to explain or justify your actions (maybe you need to make the director aware of a problem or situation), most of the time this method accomplishes little and makes you appear defensive, especially during longer note sessions when everyone is anxious to go home. Explanation serves no purpose but to prolong the notes and to aggravate your colleagues. It may feel good to let the director hear your explanation; after all, you don't want the director to think you made an ignorant choice. However, done too frequently, this makes you someone the director must "deal with" or "cut off." Most times it is best to listen to the note and respond with a simple "okay."

If you disagree with a note you are given, it is usually acceptable to either ask a question or express a differing viewpoint as part of the normal collaboration that goes on between directors and actors. Many directors expect this. If you disagree and the director stands firm, try the suggestion in good faith before forming a strong opinion. Serious disagreements are best done privately so they do not hold up rehearsal or change the atmosphere in a negative way. Rather than "fighting" a note, see if you can understand and accept the director's rationale. Can you see how the note will make the play as a whole more effective? Can you find a way to embody the note that will enhance your performance and give you some new ideas? Are you holding onto a preconceived notion of your character that is getting in your way? If none of these are true, is there a compromise you can suggest to please both the director and yourself? Remember you and the director should be on the same side with the same goal—to produce a good performance. The director is in charge, and though you want to contribute your own ideas and creativity, sometimes you must yield to a directorial decision and find a way to be at peace with it.

Try to leave your ego at home. Actors who bring their egos into the rehearsal room are usually labeled as difficult or as having an attitude. During notes, these actors put up walls and make it hard for a director to communicate with them. They may blame other actors in the cast for mishaps, regardless of whether the blame was warranted. A reluctance to accept responsibility or admit they may have failed soon becomes the habitual act of passing the buck. Nothing is ever their fault and therefore they do not have to adapt what they are doing. They may be temperamental or unwilling to hear criticism, making it an ordeal for the director to give any notes at all to them. Any actor is susceptible to trouble with ego, even well-intentioned ones. If the rehearsal is not going as you anticipated, if you are having personality conflicts with cast members or the director, or if you feel some members lack experience and you are having trouble trusting them, it is easy for your ego to start to control you. Fears and insecurities can also come into play. If you find yourself blocking or disregarding the director's notes, you need to step back and try to reframe your attitude. This will make the rehearsal process more enjoyable for you as well as for the rest of the cast.

On the other end of the scale, there are actors who see notes as a sign of failure. A note to them is taken as a criticism of their abilities and as a cause for depression. They leave rehearsal down-spirited, distraught, or emotional. These are the actors who want to be perfect, and when they are unable to meet their impossible standards, they become terribly hard on themselves. If you find yourself hearing all notes as negative, you may want to reevaluate how you perceive criticism. Whether you get a note is far from an accurate test to see if you have succeeded or failed in your attempts. A good performance is not necessarily one that doesn't generate any suggestions from the director. On the contrary, receiving notes means the director believes you are capable and skilled enough to "be directed." It may mean the director is excited by what you are doing and wants you to explore further. It certainly means he/she cares about your performance and wants you to do your best. The give-and-take, trial-and-error process is an integral part of any rehearsal—a polished performance isn't expected until the final stages. One of the rewards of being involved in an art form is the creative collaboration, and being afraid of feedback will deprive you of this privilege.

Many times actors must interpret or translate a director's notes into actable terms. Most notes demand some work on the actor's part, perhaps to integrate a new character choice or to strengthen an action. Some directors will speak about the "result" they want: "The character needs to be more worried" or "Everyone needs more energy." It is your job to find a way to get that result. What given circumstances, what action, what justification will fit into your process and yield the desired end product? As an actor, you do not merely follow instructions, you must integrate the notes into your process. When you merely try to remember all the notes and to hit every mark, you will more than likely get lost in a sea of individual details and flatten your performance.

In the course of a note session, you will probably get some praise on moments that are working well. It is certainly beneficial and reassuring for you to know you are on the right track and to have confidence in what you are doing. However, one major pitfall to this kind of reassurance is neglecting the original focus during these moments and trying to repeat the performance the director liked. These moments can become forced and lackluster, losing the spontaneity that made them successful. Rather than trying to remember what your performance was like or how it came across and then trying to recreate it, look at what you were focused on and what actions you were playing. Each performance will be different, but the action of the moment will be effective only if you trust your instincts and concentrate on what is happening in the present rather than on what happened the last time you ran the scene. Take a positive note as an opportunity to strengthen your focus.

You may find that you are not getting enough guidance. Either the director has very few notes for you in particular or has very few notes in general. This silence can be very frustrating and cause you to feel as though you are acting in a vacuum. Receiving few notes may mean you are doing fine on your own and the director trusts you. However, it may mean the director is focused on another element of the production and has not given your work equal attention. If you are not getting feedback and feel insecure about your performance, it is appropriate to solicit information directly. You might ask a general question such as, "Is my characterization on the right track?" Or you might also ask about specifics in your performance, "Am I too forceful at that moment?" or "I feel awkward sitting during that speech, does it look alright?" Get the answers you need to feel comfortable in your role.

In contrast, you may receive "notes" from sources outside your director. Friends, family, fellow cast or crew members may feel a need to express their unsolicited opinions and give you what they consider to be a little helpful direction. Listen to their advice with extreme caution. Without a full understanding of the play or the particular production, they may steer you onto the wrong course. It is the director's prerogative to make decisions about how moments are played, and it is unprofessional to replace a note from your director with one from a friend. If you want to change an element of your performance based on a suggestion you receive, *always* ask your director first. Occasionally, someone will be able to give you a helpful tip such as either identifying a line that is not understandable or letting you know you cannot be heard in a certain scene. Even this kind of information should be confirmed with your director before making any adjustments.

Note sessions can be lengthy, and you will often have to sit for long periods of time listening to notes that are not addressed to you. Patience is expected in these situations. You may find many notes, though not directed toward you specifically, can help your performance as well. Perhaps an actor is facing a situation similar to one you have in another scene. You can apply the advice to your work and save the director from repeating a note to you at a later date. As you take responsibility for your work, you will see the advantages of listening closely to all notes.

Structuring the Scene

■ Note

Energize the beginning of the scene.

Think about how the scene begins.

Attack the beginning of the scene with clarity.

The Problem

The beginning of the scene is flat, lacking the appropriate drive and energy.

Explanation

In a race, how effectively the horses come out of the starting gate determines which ones eventually succeed or fail. Likewise, how well the beginning of a scene is performed affects its overall quality. A strong beginning will engage the audience, set the tone, and start the momentum of the action. A weak one will lose the audience's interest and fail to generate the energy necessary to perpetuate the story. Some actors, overlooking the importance of these first moments, take a long time to become involved in the action; they use the beginning of a scene as a time to "gear up." Perhaps they have selected a clear action for the middle of the scene but have neglected to think about what action to start off with. Or there is the case when an actor has a quick costume change and literally has to run to place, neglecting to think about anything except getting on stage on time. This causes the scene to get off on the wrong foot, and it is difficult to recover energy and focus once the scene is underway.

Strategies

Remember the beginning of a scene is in the *middle* of your character's life. You are in the middle of a private thought, the middle of a conversation, or the middle of an action. You may have just finished one experience and are ready to start another. You may have just entered and are bringing with you certain expectations regarding what is about to transpire, or you may already have been involved in a conversation for hours. Take time to examine what has happened in your character's life before the scene begins and make choices about what is on your mind. It is often helpful to improvise what occurs in the minutes before the start of the scene. This way you have first-hand experience with the events prior to the opening line, you have made specific choices about your circumstances, and you have a firmer understanding of your state of mind.

You may have found that after you run a scene and the director immediately asks you to run it again, the second time through is significantly better. You have more energy, more focus, and are more comfortable with what you are doing. The first run may have suffered due to inadequate preparation. Warming up vocally and physically is a sure-fire way to increase your energy level. You may want to take a few private moments before you rehearse a scene to think about what has just transpired, to focus on what you want, and to remind yourself of the given circumstances. Look for a way to trigger your inner energy. Is there a visual image, a gesture, a phrase you can concentrate on which immediately drops you into the world of the play?

Additional Thoughts for the Director

Have the actors play the scene to its midpoint only; then stop them and have them begin the scene again. Coach them to take the energy they have found midway and use it as they attack the first moments of the scene. By only going to the midpoint in this exercise, you are less likely to have actors muddy the arc of the scene.

Other Notes of Interest

    Make the exposition active.

    Don't play the ending.

    Enter/exit dynamically.

■ Note

Make the exposition active.

Keep the exposition interesting.

Don't ignore the exposition.

The Problem

The exposition is uninteresting to watch and hard to follow.

Explanation

Exposition appears in virtually every play and provides the details necessary to follow what is going on. It includes character histories, past events, conflicts, details on the present situation, in other words, all the essential given circumstances. Opening scenes are traditionally the "exposition scenes," during which the basic plot information is laid out. Once we are apprised of what is happening, we are drawn into the story and anxious for the plot to develop. Though the major exposition usually occurs at the beginning of a play, background information can be revealed throughout a script. Farces or other situation comedies frequently have extensive exposition to set up comic payoffs in later scenes. In serious dramas, information may be disclosed gradually, keeping us from seeing the full picture all at once, building our tension and suspense.

Actors may want to rush through the exposition quickly, anxious to get to more dramatic or exciting moments. Getting out the facts is rarely an actor's favorite section of the play. However, if these scenes are not performed with the same energy and commitment as climactic moments, the audience may not follow the dialogue and therefore be left confused, not grasping the basic facts of the plot. If the audience is lost during the exposition, it is extremely difficult to win them over later. It is crucial for actors to approach these scenes with excitement and interest, never regarding them as insignificant.

Strategies

Information provided in exposition scenes is not only for the benefit of the audience but also for the characters. Look for reasons why you may be interested in sharing or hearing news.

- How does the news affect you? How do you want it to affect other characters?

- Does it change your opinions or plans?
- Why is it crucial information? What would you miss out on if you did not know this information?
- Why is it exciting or fascinating to you?

Remember, no fact is ordinary or unimportant because it is about the unique world in which you live. Listen to dialogue with interest and curiosity, and speak to others with purpose. If the characters are involved and moved by their conversation, it is likely that the audience will be as well. A simple exercise to accentuate this is to tell your story to a partner. After each new piece of information, have your partner react as if he is hearing a juicy bit of gossip. Have him confirm what you said with short questions (e.g., "Really?" "Is that so?" "No kidding?"). You respond affirmatively ("Yes!" "That's right!") and move on in your story. Then switch by listening to your partner's information and reacting in a similar manner. When you go back to the dialogue in context, some of the fascination will remain. As an actor, you want to enjoy and relish every scene; as a character, you want to be affected by what is said.

Opening exposition scenes can be especially difficult because some actors tend to "warm up" during the first few minutes. Ask yourself what has happened just prior to the first lines of the play. Are you in the middle of a conversation, or are you coming from another location? In rehearsal you can improvise this unwritten scene, either alone or with your fellow scene partners, then move into the actual lines of the text. This may help you find the energy and commitment necessary to keep the scene animated and interesting to play.

Additional Thoughts for the Director

Actors need to feel the information in their scene is crucial to the play as a whole. Make it a conscious decision to treat the exposition scene with as much care as the rest of the play. Otherwise, the actors may feel their scene is of less importance than other more "action-driven" scenes. If the carefree discussion between Sampson and Gregory about the feuding families in *Romeo and Juliet* is not seen as critical to the actors playing the scene, then you have no play. Strong actions will make the exposition clear and necessary to be heard.

Other Notes of Interest

Don't play the ending.
Energize the beginning of a scene.
Enter/exit dynamically.

If indeed the character has nothing other to do but to tell the other characters on stage something that has just happened, then you need to find a very strong reason to be telling it.

—Boyd Gaines

Make the exposition active, yes, as opposed to being didactic, as opposed to lecturing or worse, keeping it a secret and making the spectator guess at what's going on.

—André De Shields

■ Note

Don't play the ending.

You're getting ahead of yourself.

The Problem

The actor is allowing knowledge of how a scene or play ends to filter prematurely into the playing of a moment.

Explanation

One of the joys of watching a play is getting to know the characters and their lives, wondering what will happen to them over the course of the play, and following their ups and downs. Most of the time, we do not know what events they will encounter or how these episodes will affect them. Even when we are familiar with a play and know its conclusion, we enjoy watching the journey of the characters, seeing *how* they develop and progress from beginning to end.

The actor, having done her homework, knows how her character's attitude will change in each scene, what she will learn throughout the play, and what will be her ultimate fate. She uses this knowledge as she shapes and interprets her role, attempting to create a logical progression toward her character's eventual outcome. The danger is the actor will incorporate character developments too early in the play. For instance, she bases her first appearance as the character using information from the last scene of the play. Or an even more frequent problem, she might start a scene with the perspective and conclusions that her character reaches at the end of that same scene.

For example, the character of Scrooge in Dickens' *A Christmas Carol* begins and ends in two very different places. When we first meet him he is hard-hearted and stingy, but due to a number of ghostly visitors to his bedchamber, he becomes a much kinder and generous man. The actor playing Scrooge knows his character has a heart buried deeply underneath his gruff exterior, but if he reveals this too early he undermines the impact of the story. If in the first scene Scrooge has a charitable moment or a friendly smile, then there is no suspense. We want to watch his struggles and see his sympathetic side emerge little by little before our eyes. Likewise, the actor needs to take care not to color the beginning of a scene with the attitude the character possesses at its end. During the final moments of the scene with the Ghost of Christmas Yet to Come, Scrooge is shocked and terrified as he is shown his own grave. If he begins this scene with terror, guessing what the ghost has to show him, then there is no dramatic development. Rather he should confront the ghost with suspicion and uncertainty, arguing or pleading with it not to torment him anymore, without giving away what is about to transpire.

Strategies

As you develop your character, the key thing to remember is you are taking the audience on a journey. You want to guide them one step at a time so they can appreciate each episode of your character's life. If you skip ahead, you sacrifice the natural progression of your role and lose the audience's interest.

To avoid getting ahead of yourself, keep track of what your character knows and feels throughout the play. As you begin each scene ask yourself these questions:

- What significant events have occurred prior to this scene?
- What information does your character have as you enter the scene?
- What is your character's frame of mind at this point?

As you progress through a scene, notice the moments your character learns something.

- When does your character make a self-discovery? Learn something about others? About the situation?
- What events in the plot bring out a new aspect of your character's personality previously unnoticed by the audience?
- When does your character face a new aspect of another character's personality?

If you pinpoint the exact moment discoveries occur, you will make your scene more exciting and engaging and prevent yourself from playing the ending. As long as you move carefully through each stage of the character's life, the knowledge of the future will guide you in making choices and help you to figure out how your character gets from one moment to the next.

Additional Thoughts for the Director

A good way to help actors avoid this problem is to begin rehearsals with a discussion of the character's journey. During table readings of the script, ask actors to identify the major shifts of their characters. Follow how the shifts of one character can affect the surrounding characters. What attitudes do the characters have at the beginning of the play and what attitudes do they have at the end?

If the actor seems to have an intellectual understanding of the arc of the character, but this isn't coming across in performance, ask the actor to consider how the character develops physically and vocally. Run a scene and have the actor make specific adjustments each time the character learns something new. Also, compare how the character's energy level changes from the beginning to the ending of the scene.

Other Notes of Interest

Make the discovery.

Make the realization.

Don't play the ending, no, because then the journey is ruined. And if there's no journey, essentially there's no play. It also means stay in the moment, in the present. You must listen and watch. If you're listening and you're watching, you will not respond until you hear the important clue or cue or catalyst or trigger, and your response won't be false.

—André De Shields

This is a real stumbling block because intellectually we know what's going to happen and we start playing into it. But it is so much richer if you let the audience savor the piece until the very end. Let them be surprised, shocked, delighted.

—Karen Ziemba

■ Note

Tell the story.

Point the plot.

The Problem

The plot line is difficult to follow because of a lack of clarity on the part of the actor.

Explanation

At its very foundation, theatre is a form of storytelling. An audience comes to hear and see a story brought to life before them. No matter how brilliant the acting or how beautiful the scenery, if the audience cannot follow the plot they will be frustrated and lose interest. Actors and directors have a responsibility to make sure—regardless of their concept, design, or interpretation—the basic story line is accessible.

This is not always easy to do. Texts with complicated plots or unfamiliar language, such as Shakespeare, present special challenges and demand extra effort from the performers. But, if not played clearly, even straightforward plays can be difficult to follow. It is unwise to take for granted that the audience will automatically grasp the information they need.

By the time an audience arrives, actors are very familiar with the script and can probably recite each others' lines as well as their own. If someone rushes a line or mumbles a name, fellow actors have no trouble following what was said. But since audience members are hearing and seeing everything for the first time, lost lines can create a confusion that could last from a few seconds to the entire length of the play. Even if just one crucial bit of information is muddied it can cause a multitude of whispers: "What did he say?" "What's going on?" "I missed that." To prevent this situation, actors need to give attention to highlighting and clarifying plot elements.

Strategies

Telling the story is important throughout the play, from the exposition to the final moments. Every scene reveals something that concerns the characters, their relationships, their intentions, and their discoveries. No matter what your interpretation, the basic facts stay the same. Boil down each scene and determine what it is really about. Summarize that central action in a brief sentence. Is it a betrayal, a flirtation, a confrontation, a misunderstanding? Look for the major events; how does the scene progress from one point to the next? Ask yourself what pieces of plot information are absolutely fundamental for the audience to know to follow the story. Once you are aware of what needs to be communicated, you will be more likely to make intelligent choices and keep the plot in focus.

Vocal clarity is a sure-fire way to help the story line remain clear, and strong projection and articulation are your most significant tools. Establish a regular vocal warm-up and check with your director periodically as to whether you can be heard and understood. If you say a key piece of information for the first time—a name, a fact, a new circumstance—you can highlight it through vocal emphasis. If your character reveals he is planning a murder, you certainly want the audience to hear the word "murder." Increase your volume, change your pitch or inflection, or linger longer on the word; use whatever technique suits the action of your character. When you vary your vocal quality, you catch the audience's ear and grab their attention.

You can convey the story through your physical choices as well. An important statement can be accentuated through a turn, a gesture, a moment of stillness, or simply by looking another character in the eye. Just as you do not want to rush through a line, you do not want to rush through a physical moment. A glance between characters may be the perfect way to establish they are conspiring together, but if it is done too quickly or while other action is happening, it can be lost. A movement can be too subtle and need enhancement. For instance, if a smile of support is not large enough to be read by an audience, try a more eye-catching move such as a pat on the back. The audience should have a good idea of what is going on by watching the stage pictures adjust from one moment to the next, even if they cannot hear the dialogue.

Additional Thoughts for the Director

Watch a run-through of a scene as an "innocent," as if you had never seen the play before. Clear your mind of expectations and try not to be distracted by details of the performances. Listen simply for the story. Are any words being lost or ideas being muddied? Is the plot being clearly set up? Does one plot point lead logically into the next? An audience needs guidance. Think of the play as a road map toward a destination. Clarify all the turns and forks in the road. When does the character make a decision that alters the expected course? Signpost those plot shifts.

To help determine if the story is being told visually, use the snap shot test. Each time there is a physical move or adjusted position, take a mental picture. Ask yourself these questions:

- Is the composition capturing what is happening in that moment?
- Is the distance between characters appropriate? Does it represent the energy or tension in their relationships?

- Is there a physical as well as dramatic progression to the scene?
- Are key moments in focus? Are there too many moves blurring that focus? Or does there need to be a bigger movement to take that focus?

Other Notes of Interest

Emphasize key words.

Give focus/take focus.

■ Note

Trust the text.

Don't impose on the text.

The Problem

The actor's interpretation of the text is overly complicated.

Explanation

Many brilliant actors are identified with their signature characters, for instance, Marlon Brando as Stanley Kowalski, Sarah Bernhardt as Camille, or John Barrymore as Hamlet. These actors have put a unique stamp on their roles, and their performances are celebrated as singular achievements. Every actor strives to create a memorable performance, one that is noteworthy and special.

This urge to be special may challenge an actor to work doubly hard and lead to exciting and insightful discoveries about the character. However, it also may lead an actor down a less profitable path. In this second case, the actor approaches the script thinking, "What can I *do* with this role? How can I make it unique? What will make my performance more impressive?" Thus, the actor's first priority becomes to find something clever to add to the role to make the interpretation stand out. She wants to do *more* than what the text offers, which may lead her to create double meanings where they do not exist, use extraneous movement, or embellish the character with traits that are not justified by the script. For instance, the actor may take a straightforward accusation the character delivers and fill it with doubts and struggle the playwright did not intend. Or she may come up with intricate mannerisms for a moment when her character is simply reacting to being rejected by her lover.

The actor's focus has moved from finding what is interesting *in the text*, to how she can be interesting *herself*. Unadorned, truthful choices are avoided in favor of elaborate and complicated ones. The actor works hard to be memorable, rather than relaxing into the role and trusting that simplicity will be interesting enough.

Strategies

What makes a performance memorable is usually not what you add to the text but how clearly and powerfully you are able to embody it. Once you let go of the need to devise a clever interpretation of your role and have taken this pressure off yourself, you can turn your attention to investigating what material the playwright has given you. You will find there are infinite choices offered by the script, and many layers of your character to unearth. Letting the text guide you does not mean you limit your creativity; it often opens you up to deeper, more profound possibilities. This can lead you to an inspired and unique interpretation of your role.

As you make decisions regarding your character, ask yourself the following:

- Does your idea spring from the text?
- What evidence in the text supports your choice? Justify your choice with specific lines or actions.
- Does your choice reveal something about your character?
- Are you looking for what a line *could* mean (inventing interpretations) rather than for what it *does* mean?

Be strict with yourself and put each idea to the test. The more you examine the text and discover its truths, the more you will appreciate the playwright's intent.

Additional Thoughts for the Director

When an actor unnecessarily embellishes choices, this is a signal she may be insecure—worried her performance is not interesting enough. The first step is to reassure her and dispel her fears. Tell the actor what is working in her performance, why you cast her, or how her unique qualities especially complement the role. Sincerity is important; if you praise an aspect of her performance you secretly believe is weak, the actor may sense this and withdraw her trust. Help her to relax in the role and let her see that she doesn't need to work so hard to succeed.

You can also aid the actor by helping to clarify and simplify her choices. If a moment is complicated or confused, ask the actor, "What did you intend here?" If her intention does not match her performance, point this out. "That's great, but that is not what is coming across. From the audience's perspective, this is what I am getting..." Or, "I'm not able to follow that moment because I am distracted by..." Let her know which choices are working and compliment them, then point out how extraneous choices detract from what is effective.

Other Notes of Interest

> Go back to your script.
>
> Tell the story.
>
> You are working too hard.

■ Note

Build the sequence or speech.

The Problem

A heightened moment in a scene is lacking vocal and emotional builds.

Explanation

In a piece of music, it is the dynamics that catch our interest and drive the momentum forward. A composer can grab our attention, build our suspense, or keep us on the edge of our seats through the use of pitch, tempo, and intensity. If the builds and the crescendos are ignored and the performance remains at one level, the emotional impact of the music is sacrificed and we quickly tune out. Just as with music, scripts have inherent dynamics which the playwright uses to highlight moments and to keep the audience engaged.

When a scene feels flat and lacks momentum, it may be because the builds in the script have been neglected. Some moments demand increasing intensity, on both a vocal and an emotional level, to set them apart and to give them power. In a build, each idea has more excitement than the one that precedes it, and this peaks our interest for the one that follows. There is a sense of growing tension about what will be said next. Of course it is always important to keep a scene moving forward; builds are not unique in this regard. However, there is a heightened quality to builds that makes them more distinctive and powerful. If you were to graph the scene, the builds are the high points, the peaks, that keep the graph from being a straight line. The audience needs to feel the energy of these moments and be drawn in by them.

Strategies

To identify builds, look for the progression of ideas in a scene. Find the points where people's views clash, the conflict increases, and decisions need to be made. Is there a sense that something is about to happen, that a change is near? A build leads into this change. It may precede a victory or loss for your character, a revelation, a resolution, or especially—a new action. The intensity of the action surges to a climax and then decreases to begin a new progression. A build may either exist in a monologue or, as is most often the case, be shared among several actors. You may find it helpful to mark your script: number items in lists, highlight ideas you use to make your case, underline ideas that are compared or contrasted. This will help you to see the thought process of your character.

If a build is not coming naturally, play the moment in isolation and experiment with increasing the intensity of your performance. Think of climbing a mountain; as you go higher and higher, it takes more energy, strength, and resolve. Work toward the goal of reaching the top and toward the sense of fulfillment and accomplishment you experience when you succeed. Go overboard and find the extremes in your actions and reactions. If you feel an emotion surfacing, follow it to its limits, even if it seems illogical. Do not restrain your impulses; now is the time to open the floodgates to see what happens. Let your vocal power build as the sequence progresses. With each new idea, add more volume, more intensity, and a deeper connection to your breath. Commit fully to the importance of what you are saying and make sure you communicate your meaning to others. You may experience surges of energy and moments of regrouping, small peaks and valleys on your journey to the top. When the build reaches its peak, you should feel at your vocal and emotional peak as well. After this experimentation, step back and evaluate what you discovered.

- Did you sense the momentum and upward drive of the sequence or speech?
- Did you find your commitment to the ideas grew?
- Did you find an emotional connection to what you were saying?
- Did the increase of vocal power help in building toward the climax?

This kind of work usually does not need to be repeated; if done too often it may lead to indulgent and overplayed acting. Note your insights and let them inform your next rehearsal. Find the intensity of the build and then play it at a level appropriate to the style of the script.

Additional Thoughts for the Director

While this note can be given to an individual with a complicated build in the dialogue, remember there are also difficult sequences in a play that will involve the entire group on stage. This is especially true in the final scene of a Shakespeare play, an intense moment in a courtroom drama, a family confrontation, or public events, such as an auction or prayer meeting. A good analogy to use is a tour of passengers on a ride down the rapids. Everyone has a collective stake in the outcome of the trip: to make it through treacherous waters and arrive safely without capsizing the boat. The importance of working as a team should be stressed. Remember as you build the sequence, to take the time to focus individual as well as collective responses to the action.

Other Notes of Interest

Build vocally.

You are holding back emotionally.

■ Note

Separate your thoughts.

You are generalizing.

The Problem

The actor is running ideas together and not working through each thought individually.

Explanation

A good playwright will build layers of meaning into a script. The more deeply an actor studies a script, the more the actor will find nuances in the thought process of the character. Part of the excitement of working on a part is discovering, investigating, and highlighting the twists and turns taken by the character. Not all these thoughts will be apparent at first. Actors start their work with a general understanding of a scene. They know the main ideas, the beginning and ending points for their characters, and more or less what their lines mean. But, if actors stop here, they will miss much of the richness in the script.

Without careful attention to all the details in the text, an actor can speed through a speech, skipping some thoughts and blending others together. The actor may know the final idea of a line and play that conclusion rather than move through each step in progression. This problem occurs quite often with long or complex speeches. The actor plays the speech as one big chunk; thus, all the lines end up having the same general meaning or worse, no meaning at all. If actors don't fully understand the significance of what they are saying, they may run through words too quickly, without giving them any inflection or importance. This can happen with not only long passages, but also any time two or more ideas exist in a line together.

Strategies

To help you slow down and identify each thought individually, try experimenting with adverbs. As an exercise, take each new thought and say it with a distinct quality. For example, say the first thought sternly, the next sweetly, the next flirtatiously, the next directly. This will separate the ideas in a technical fashion and allow you to sense how each idea stands alone. Also look at the progression of ideas and feel how each one leads you forward.

Once you have done this, focus on communicating to the other people on stage. How can each idea help you to get other characters to understand your point of view? Lead them through your thought process, take them one step at a time, and make them see what you are thinking and feeling. Each thought changes and develops your main idea. You may not know what conclusion you'll reach by the end of the speech, so take it moment by moment, don't get ahead of yourself, and lead them through your thinking.

The danger is, in your effort to recognize each idea, that you can end up giving all your thoughts equal weight. Consequently, your speech plays at just one level and becomes difficult to follow. Instead, sort through and evaluate your ideas as you go along. Look for what is important and what is superficial. Some thoughts you may want to emphasize or linger on; others may serve as quick steps getting you closer to the crux of your argument. Choose your battles.

Additional Thoughts for the Director

A good playwright works painstakingly to find the right words for the right moment. A good way to find out how well the actors understand the thoughts of a speech, is to have them, in their own words, paraphrase the lines of the text. In this manner, you will be sure they know what they are saying and that important information isn't being glossed over or altogether lost. If an actor has a particularly long and revealing passage, help to clarify the main idea in the text that fuels the rest of the speech.

Other Notes of Interest

Don't play the ending.

Don't rush.

Find the antithesis.

Build the sequence or speech.

Separate your thoughts. Especially when an actor has a speech and he thinks it's one thing, have him treat the monologue like a dialogue. How is a monologue a dialogue with yourself? How are you arguing with yourself? How do you put forward ideas? You want to find the rhythm of a tennis match, just as you do in a dialogue.

—Bill Rauch

■ Note

Make the transition.

The Problem

The actor needs to find a bridge between two consecutive, but distinct, actions.

Explanation

In many ways, a play is a journey for a character. As he moves from one point in his life to another, he encounters a series of circumstances that cause him to change, grow, and take action. A fully developed character will have many shifts, twists, and turns throughout the course of the play; it is these changes that make the character interesting to watch. Even within one scene, a character will usually move through several actions. Each change represents a thought and decision on the part of the character.

In realistic acting, there is a connection from one action to the next. One moment propels you into the next, just as it has grown out of the previous one. When an actor jumps from idea to idea without finding a link between them, his lines become choppy and hard to follow. Without the connections between moments, without the inner thoughts and decisions, there are gaps or breaks in the reality of the character's journey. It is as though he were traveling on one path and then suddenly appears on a new path, without the audience being able to see the turn or know how he got there. This can lead to confusion or, worse, to the audience losing interest in the character. There is also a lack of dramatic tension when the character skips from moment to moment without any struggle or consideration. Finding the transitions from one action to the next is crucial to making a character three-dimensional and consistent.

Strategies

Analyzing the structure of a scene is a good place to start when working on character transitions. Look for the shifts and changes, where the character moves from one action to another. This is often called finding the beats. Here are some places where transitions usually occur:

- when the topic of a conversation shifts
- when significant new information is introduced
- when one character accomplishes an action
- when a decision is made
- when the circumstances change
- when another character enters or exits
- when the action is interrupted
- when the playwright suggests a pause

Usually, if you pay attention to the natural rhythm of a scene, your instincts will tell you where these shifts occur.

Once you have identified where your character begins a new action, you can begin to examine the transition. How do you get from one point to another? What runs through your mind? Do you weigh any options? Is it an easy shift or a struggle? How does the new action relate to the moment before? What physical movement or vocal changes occur? Look also at the tempo of your character. Some characters process information quickly and spontaneously; others may do so slowly.

For example, let's say your character moves from accusing a friend of betraying a secret, to apologizing to him for jumping to conclusions. Creating a bridge between these two contrasting actions will allow the audience to follow your character's train of thought, and probably help them to relate to him as well. What feeling, response, or information triggers your character to stop accusing his friend? What does he think about in the time before he begins to apologize? Is he struggling with his emotions? Does he move away from or toward his friend? Does he change his tone of voice? As he begins to speak, is he trying to make up for his accusations?

Transitions are important in telling the story of a character, but they do not need to be overplayed or prolonged. You don't want to pause and think, "Now I'll play my transition." They serve as bridges from moment to moment, not as stopping points. As you rehearse a scene, you may want to play your transitions slowly to fully understand each stage of your character's actions. However, once you are able to grasp the thought process of your character, condense the time these shifts take. Transitions are part of the action and should not slow down the momentum of the performance.

Additional Thoughts for the Director

If a scene seems flat and missing transitions, rehearse each "beat" separately. Work to frame moments through clear physical and vocal choices. Examine what is at stake in each beat and how it differs from the beats preceding and following it. Experiment with different tactics and actions. Then go back and run the entire scene, paying close attention to whether there is an interesting progression of events and the story is being told.

If a transition is muddy, you can have the actors speak their subtext or inner monologue aloud. This forces the actors to articulate their thought process. Sometimes this alone solves the problem, and it allows you to check if the actors' choices are moving the action forward.

Other Notes of Interest

Don't play the ending.

Make the realization.

Separate your thoughts.

Transitions are the breath of a play. They are what make a play undulate; they make a play pulsate. The exact opposite of that is what happens on television or in many films, that smash cutting thing: boom! boom! boom! boom! No wonder we don't have attention spans anymore. That's one of the beauties of the theatre; we have to pay attention to the journey.

—André De Shields

■ Note

Find the action when telling a story about the past.

Don't get lost in the past.

The Problem

The actor is delivering a story about the past without a clear action that is relevant to the present moment.

Explanation

Actors are often faced with monologues that retell events from a character's past. Many playwrights use long speeches at key moments in a play to explain a character's background or behavior. If you flip through a script and look for a long passage, more than likely it will be a story written in the past tense. Actors searching for audition monologues frequently are drawn to these kinds of speeches because they are the appropriate length and have a clear beginning, middle, and end. Though these passages can recount fascinating stories and reveal important information about a character, they also can be acting traps. If done poorly, a past-tense speech can stop the action of the play, put the character relationships and objectives on hold, and contribute nothing to the advancement of the plot. In auditions, it is more difficult to highlight acting skills using a past-tense monologue, for many actors get caught in merely reciting a good story rather than engaging in a dynamic moment in a character's life.

Just as an exposition scene is challenging to make interesting, stories about the past are tricky to deliver because nothing appears to be happening in the present moment. The purpose of the speech seems to be "to inform the audience about what has occurred before the play began," certainly not a very intriguing objective. It is tempting for the actor to be drawn into remembering and recounting a story, forgetting about the here and now while reliving a past event. So absorbed in the past, she disconnects from the other characters on stage. This can be avoided if the actor determines why the story is relevant to the immediate moment and finds a clear action to play.

Strategies

First, it is crucial to decide why your character is telling her story at that specific moment. A story may be either about a difficult or especially vulnerable time in a character's life or about a highpoint or peak experience. Whatever the case, there is a trigger, a special reason why a character needs to reveal something about her past. Determine the following:

- What event or piece of dialogue causes your character to open up? Find the specific moment when you decide to speak.

- What do you want to accomplish by telling the story? Avoid objectives such as "to relive the moment" or "to remember the past." Rather, pick an objective that is connected to the present and to the other people in the scene.

- How do you want to affect whomever you are speaking to? How do you want them to react? What do you need to get them to do?

- Why do you choose to relate your story to this person(s). What do you want them to think about you? How is this a turning point in your relationship?

As you rehearse with the other actors, look for the changes in the dynamics of your relationship. In other words, what is happening between you and your scene partners *as you tell the story?* What reactions and realizations do you or others have while you speak, and how do they change the way you finish the story? What adjustments in posture, facial expression, tone of voice, or timing do you have to make as you go along? How does your relationship grow or develop by the end of the story? If you have trouble answering these questions, imagine what the play would be like if the story was removed. What would be missing? How would the action of the play be crippled by its absence? What link does the story provide that keeps the play moving forward?

Once you have determined why you are telling the story, use the words in the monologue to accomplish your objective. Actors frequently get lost in the images of a well-written story, indulging in the feelings these images evoke and listening to the sound of their own voices. Needless to say, this stops the action of the play. Remind yourself that the words have a purpose and can help you to achieve what you want from the scene. Look for specific words and phrases that might support your objective; find the power in the language. Employ your words to affect and change the other characters in the scene.

Additional Thoughts for the Director

Work with the actor to strengthen her relationship with the other character(s) in the scene. This can be accomplished by having her upgrade her objective both before and after her telling of the story. Playwrights traditionally place stories from a character's past at critical junctures in the scene or play. Have the actor focus her attention on the "build-up" to the telling of the story and then have her place a greater weight on what happens directly after it has been told. By asking the actor to play a stronger sense of anticipation and then excitement over the outcome of the scene, you will help her find why the story is so critical to the action of the play.

Also work with the actors who listen to the story and help them to intensify their responses, giving the storyteller more to play off of. At first, have the actors exaggerate their reactions to help clarify where they occur as well as to provoke the storyteller to be clear. After everyone has a firm understanding of the give and take between the storyteller and the listeners, tone down the responses to a more realistic level so as not to steal focus from the storyteller and the story.

Other Notes of Interest

Raise the stakes.

Make the exposition active.

■ Note

Make the realization.

Draw the conclusion.

Add it up.

The Problem

The actor is underplaying or ignoring a moment of realization for the character.

Explanation

It is rare that a person either makes a major decision or forms a final opinion about something after having only one piece of information. It usually takes much more time to decide or even to recognize that a decision needs to be made. We go through life-absorbing facts and opinions through our experiences and through hearing the experiences of others. This information floats around in the back of our minds until either we are ready to assimilate it or, more often, until we are confronted by an event that forces us to deal with it. In these important moments, ideas come together in new ways, we process things for the first time, and we come to realizations. Naturally it is exciting and revealing for the audience to watch characters in these moments because they are allowed to share in their growth and insights.

The audience expects to see this in murder mysteries. At the beginning of a mystery, all a detective knows is a random number of facts that do not point to any murderer. Gradually he collects clues, observes scenes, and encounters suspects, absorbing information as he goes along. Eventually a moment comes when all the evidence begins to show a pattern and the detective is able to put the pieces together into a coherent solution. These same stages—collecting information over time, processing it, and making a realization—occur in almost every play.

Strategies

Although major realizations are often near the climax of the play, a character may draw a significant conclusion at any time during the story. If you are not immediately able to identify where your character's realizations are, look for changes in your character's outlook. At the beginning of the play ask yourself:

- What do you want?
- How do you think you will proceed?
- What do you believe about others?
- Whom do you trust?

If any of your answers change by the end of the play, search for when the switch occurs. Are there moments of confusion or confrontation that build toward your character's need to make a decision? Are there experiences or revelatory facts that can serve as triggers? Once you have found these points in the script, then you can layer them into your character's thought process. The following five steps are typical:

1. Hear/receive the information that serves as a trigger.
2. Add it up.
3. Come to a new understanding: the "aha!" moment.

4. Make a decision.

5. Act on the decision.

Clarifying each step will help the audience understand the journey of your character. In rehearsal, go through them one at a time, slowly, making sure you understand the logical progression from one step to the next. Once you have made the realization process part of your character, then you can follow the natural rhythm of the moment. Some of the steps may happen simultaneously, or they may occur gradually, over the length of a scene.

Additional Thoughts for the Director

Side coaching can help actors to clarify and strengthen their choices. Have the actors play the scene without stopping while you verbally encourage them. Use simple positive phrases, coaxing the actors to commit to what they are doing. Your goal is to point out key moments to them, help them to follow their impulses, and to energize their actions. Possible interjections might include:

- Listen to that.
- Let that hit you.
- Add it up.
- Yes!
- Go for it.
- Don't hold back.

Other Notes of Interest

Make the discovery.

Don't play the ending.

■ Note

Finish the scene.

Put a cap on it.

The Problem

The scene lacks a strong ending.

Explanation

The old adage "leave them wanting more" is a philosophy that applies not only to good playwriting but also to strong acting. We strive in the theatre to draw the audience into the story and to keep them hooked until the end. Experienced playwrights structure their plays so the final moment of each scene leaves the audience anxious to know what will happen next. Just as a good novel is a "page turner," a good actor knows how to finish a scene giving the audience a sense of anticipation.

Most scenes in a play can be divided into units of action, or as Stanislavsky termed them, beats. At the end of each beat, the characters either achieve their objectives for the moment or come to a point where they need to regroup, rethink, or intensify what they will try next. The last beat of a scene is especially important, as it makes a final statement about what has just happened and gives us an idea about what we can expect next. Ending a scene on a strong note is called "putting a cap on it." This indicates a closure, but like a lid on a container that still has something good left in it, it is sealed up but ready to be reopened at the appropriate time.

Strategies

If you are having trouble putting a cap on a scene, it may be the moment is feeling unfinished to you. It is desirable to deliver your last line with a sense of finality, so the audience is aware that the scene has come to an end. If you are ending a conversation, try using a downward inflection and driving your energy to the very last word in the line. Practice this by saying your line and then adding at the end: "and that is all I have to say about it." Keep using this technique until you find the right commitment and feel for the ending line, and then delete the added words. Sometimes the cap of a scene may not be a line of dialogue but a strongly executed movement such as an exit, a gesture, a collapse, a kiss, or a door slam. Just as you want to speak the last line with energy and commitment, the last movement also needs a strong finish.

If your character ends the scene with a sense of satisfaction, it might be useful to think of it as a dart game. There are a series of hits and misses in the game, but you are always aiming for the bull's-eye. Every time you make a point, mark it with a slash in your script. When you finally hit the bull's-eye, mark the moment with a star. Now go back and play the scene, layering in your dart throws. Feel the satisfaction of the bull's-eye when you finish the line that you starred, and relish the moment for a minute before you go on.

Additional Thoughts for the Director

A good exercise to try is called "framing." Framing means to break the scene down into its various pictures. As you work through a scene, find those important relational moments between characters that you want to highlight as a "still picture" for the audience. Have the actors adjust themselves physically to make the strongest statement possible. Ask several questions:

- What is the distance between the actors?
- What is the tension line?
- What are the levels and planes?
- Are they facing away from each other? Toward one another? Or is only one actor facing away?

Continue through the scene, stopping and starting as you clarify the endings of each beat or unit. Give the last frame of the scene a sense of finality. Go back and run the sequence, having the actors pause after each framed moment. Then go back once more and take out all the pauses. This will aid in creating a strong pace, while helping the actors to put the endings in the right places.

If you are working on the type of play that is structured for applause at the end of scenes, acts, or musical numbers, and you are not getting the applause, this is a good indicator the audience does not understand something is over. Work with the actors to strengthen final lines and movements, and coordinate these with lighting and sound cues.

Other Notes of Interest

Make the transition.

Enter/exit dynamically.

Drive energy through to the end of the line.

It has something to do with closure, with making things finite. One of the important elements of any storytelling is reconciliation. And finishing the scene has a lot to do with reconciliation. The crux of the play is based on conflict, the resolution of the play is based on reconciliation. You can't finish the scene without at least those two basics. Conflict is where the drama comes from and the resolution or the denouement comes from things being reconciled—or not being reconciled.

—André De Shields

The Notes

Vocal Clarity

■ Note

Emphasize key words.

Use operative words.

The Problem

The actor's lines are lacking emphasis and are hard to understand.

Explanation

During the course of a play an audience will hear thousands of words without much time to mull them over and with no opportunity to ask actors to repeat words they might have missed. If no particular words "jump out" and catch the attention of the listener, lines begin to blend together. A series of flat lines soon becomes a blur of words without meaning. Even if an actor is articulating and projecting, he will not necessarily be understandable. It is therefore the burden of the actor to help the audience catch the essential ideas of the play at first hearing, by highlighting the most important words through emphasis. When we hear the significant words, it is easier for us to follow the plot.

The words that carry the most meaning in a sentence are called the "key" or "operative" words. Key words are usually nouns (the subjects) and verbs (the actions); they express who is doing what. For example, in the line "Arise, fair sun, and kill the envious moon," the nouns and verbs are: arise, sun, kill, and moon. Those four words provide the essential meaning of the line. If these words are emphasized, it is likely that the audience will listen to and comprehend what is being said. In fact, if the audience were *only* to catch these key words, they still would have a chance of following what was going on. Adjectives and pronouns are not typically emphasized unless in a comparison: The house was *green*, not yellow. *I* ran much faster than he did.

Strategies

Spending time with the text is essential. Analyze and identify the ideas and actions of your character. Once this is done, important words and phrases will be much easier to determine. Read the text aloud and concentrate solely on meaning rather than on acting. Look for the words that most effectively communicate your character's goals. The more familiar you are with your script, the more comfortable you will be in speaking your lines.

Some technical work can be helpful. Take a difficult passage of your script and underline or highlight the key words; this will remind you to consistently emphasize those words. *Arise*, fair *sun*, and *kill* the envious *moon*. Start by considering which words are crucial to the message—if you were to send a telegram, when you have to pay for every word you include, which words would be absolutely essential to communicate your thought? Then determine their relative priority, remembering that the nouns and verbs are usually the most important.

Adjectives will often seem as significant, but they will be understood without special emphasis. By stressing the noun they modify, adjectives are made clear. (For example, in the sentence, "The rabid dog will bite," only *dog* and *bite* need emphasis. The word *rabid* will be heard in relationship to *dog*, the word it describes, and therefore needs no extra punch.) Emphasizing too many adjectives and pronouns will create an awkward rhythm of speech and often make it harder to hear the nouns and verbs.

This is not to suggest, however, there is a hard and fast rule as to which words should be emphasized. Identifying all your nouns and verbs is an excellent start, but not all these words necessarily deserve equal weight. Some nouns may be more important than others. It is possible that some pronouns and adjectives will need emphasis, as might other parts of speech (adverbs, prepositions, etc.). As you get to know your script and your character, it will become clearer which words need an extra *punch*. Your director may want certain words to be stressed. Your character's relationship to other characters may dictate some of your choices. The context and the situation may suggest the importance of certain ideas, or your character may need a specific word to drive home a point. Let your analysis and instinct guide your selection. If in doubt, however, choose the nouns and verbs.

A key word needs to stand out in relation to the words around it. It needs to catch the ear of the audience. Several vocal techniques can be used to set apart a key word. Here are a few options:

- Punch the volume of the word.
- Raise its pitch.
- Spend more time on the word.
- Elongate its vowels.
- Change its inflection.
- Give the word a strong vocal attack.
- Lower its volume (still keeping it audible).
- Lower its pitch.

Additional Thoughts for the Director

You may find an "in-the-dark" rehearsal useful. Have the actors spread out around the entire room and turn out the lights. Now play the scene listening carefully for emotional connection to key words. When the connection does not seem clear, have the actor stop and go back until he *needs* the word, and needs to *send it out* to the other characters.

If the actors are playing a fairly intimate scene and are shy about emphasizing words, have them play the scene imagining they are separated by a large canyon or river. Then allow them to get close again, but retaining this distance in their minds.

You can get actors involved in the power of their words by having them take a scene and select the ten (or other reasonable number) most important words they say. Now play the scene having the actors taking turns, saying only one word at a time. The words need not be said in the order they appear in the text, or even make sense as dialogue. This will help you to find what words the actors have chosen as important to their characters and which words they have left out. After this exercise, go back and play the scene and see if the key words now have more impact.

You can test whether the sense of a scene is being communicated by trying to hear it as a first-time listener. To the best of your ability, clear your mind of your expectations and knowledge of the play and just listen to the words. You may want to look away from the stage or close your eyes. Which words are you missing? What lacks emphasis? What can't you follow? Is the story being told?

Other Notes of Interest

> Don't overstress words.
>
> Tell the story.

■ Note

> Drive energy through to the end of the line.
>
> Drive to the end of the thought.
>
> Avoid falling sentences.
>
> Avoid end-dropping.

The Problem

The tail end of a sentence falls in pitch, energy, and volume.

Explanation

Falling inflections are common in conversational speech patterns. Sitting a few feet away from others, a person does not have to worry about her voice carrying or her energy projecting. In fact, many people tend to drop volume at the end of sentences or tone down their voices so as not to be perceived as overly aggressive.

Sentences with dwindling energy may be common in casual conversation, but they do not translate well onto the stage. Unfortunately, falling sentences are a habitual problem for many performers. For an actor to be heard and keep the attention of the audience, the lines must have energy from beginning to end. Actors who habitually drop the ends of their sentences are likely to fall into a monotone rhythm, lack a sense of build or momentum in their speech, and lose the interest of the audience. Even more, when the final word or phrase fades out, the meaning of the sentence is often lost, leaving the audience straining to hear and understand. Instead of one sentence or idea propelling itself forward into the next, the energy is continually dropped and no sense of flow develops.

Strategies

A typical English sentence is structured with the significant information or meaning placed at the end. In the sentence, "The jewels are hidden in the vase," the word *vase* is what the audience is waiting to hear. If an audience member misses this word they are frustrated and may even lean over to the person next to them to ask what the actor said. Identify the last important word or phrase, frequently it is the very last word of the sentence, and underline it. If you keep in mind how important this information is and emphasize it, the ideas being communicated will not be lost and the falling inflection will naturally disappear.

You can work technically to break a habit of falling sentences by practicing other inflection patterns. Rather than letting the energy drop on the last few words of a sentence, try staying on a constant pitch to make a firm statement with the line. Imagining an exclamation point at the end of the sentence may help you to get the feel of this. Also try some upward inflections, letting the pitch rise at the end of a sentence. This technique can also add variety to your speech, though too many upward inflections will not be effective, as they tend to sound like questions.

Getting physically involved with the words is also an effective rehearsal technique. Find a strong movement such as throwing your arms forward, throwing a ball, running, or stamping your foot on the floor—and do this action at the tail end of each sentence. Think about sending your message to your scene partner as you do your movement. This will energize your words. Rather than pulling back from the ideas at the end of a line, you physically send them forward.

Additional Thoughts for the Director

Avoid making this note too general, i.e., "You have a falling sentence problem throughout the entire play." This can overwhelm an actor and unintentionally make the problem worse. Give the actor specific sentences and words in the text you feel are not carrying the intent of the character. Encourage her to send the message to other characters through the force of her will and by a conviction to what she is saying. Intensifying the commitment can often energize the full line.

Other Notes of Interest

Emphasize key words.

Clean up your diction.

Tell the story.

■ Note

Build vocally.

Use topping and undercutting.

The Problem

An exchange of lines is lacking excitement and is vocally flat.

Explanation

When an exchange in the dialogue demands extra intensity in the delivery, actors often turn to a technique called topping. Topping is a sequence of vocal builds in which one character responds to what he hears by trying to outdo or "one-better" his partner(s). The pitch of the dialogue goes up a notch with each response, so as the exchange gets more and more exciting, the pitch gets higher and higher. Eventually the sequence or competition reaches its height and can go no further. The final line can be the peak of the build, or it can be delivered as an undercut, dropping down in pitch and delivering the final blow or last word. This can happen either once or a number of times in one scene. There may be several sequences in a row, such as in a comic stichomythia.

Comedians have long known about the technique of topping and undercutting. When a routine involves one-upmanship, professional comics will set up their lines clearly and carefully. They draw us in, build our interest, create excitement, and then come in with the punch line. Dramatic dialogue also benefits from vocal and emotional builds. When ideas grow in urgency or importance, a vocal crescendo amplifies their power and impact. Topping is easily applied to quick exchanges of dialogue such as arguments, accusations, competitions, or moments of panic, when ideas are coming at a rapid-fire pace. When properly used, topping and undercutting can energize lines, clean up timing, and make a scene more effective.

Strategies

The keys to successful topping and undercutting are teamwork and concentration. You must listen to your partners, let their lines feed into yours, and respond quickly. Usually, each piece of dialogue in a topping sequence comes directly after its cue line; pauses are seldom used because they slow down the momentum. Sometimes you will find that you challenge a partner by repeating a word or phrase he has just said. For example, "I told you, you were *wrong*." "What do you mean *wrong!*" Underline the words in your script, listen for your partner to say them, and punch them in your reply.

Pitch is a crucial element in topping sequences. If the pitch of each line stays at the same level, there is no increase in the excitement.

Rehearse the sequence concentrating solely on climbing up the ladder of notes. You can use a piano or even sing the lines to help solidify the build. The first line in the exchange must start low enough so there is room to grow, and you must listen carefully to the pitch of the line preceding yours. If the sequence is long, you need to pace yourself. Do not get too high too fast or you will hit the top of your range before the exchange is finished. However, do not limit yourself to the normal notes of your speaking voice. The highs and lows will probably reach beyond your accustomed range. Good breath support is essential.

Topping also requires you to deliver your lines with a strong conviction. As your character, you must believe you *need* to be heard. Your responses are more significant, better phrased, more forceful, or even cleverer than what you just heard. Select strong actions, reinforcing the importance of what you have to say, such as to win, to cajole, to enlighten, to mock, to taunt, to brag, to incite, to provoke, to demand, or to pressure. Finally, remember to enjoy the exchange and deliver your lines with finesse.

Additional Thoughts for the Director

Practice makes perfect. Once a sequence of builds has been layered into the scene, remind the actors that the technical side of their work should be invisible to the audience. Though you need to practice a tricky sequence over and over to achieve the appropriate timing, you want the actor's work to appear believable and not mechanical. A good phrase for the actors to keep in mind is "never let 'em see you sweat."

Other Notes of Interest

Build the sequence or speech.

■ Note

Don't overstress words.

You are hitting every word.

Too many words have equal weight.

The Problem

Too many words are being emphasized, causing a speech to lose its effectiveness.

Explanation

Though emphasizing important words is crucial in helping to clarify meaning, an actor can overdo it. Some actors, full of energy and good intentions, attack their lines and punch every noun, verb, and adjective they encounter. They may feel as though they are really working the speech, really articulating the story or their intention in order to make the text especially clear. However, the result is that the audience is assaulted with emphasis; they are showered with too many ideas and are given no help in sorting them out. The audience may be led to focus on the delivery and the technique of the actor rather than on what she is saying, which in turn draws the audience away from the story and leaves them confused. Overstressing words can also be a symptom of a lack of clarity on the part of the actor—either she isn't sure of the point of her speech, or she has not identified the objective of the character. When an actor fully grasps the intent of the character, she will also intuit which words have the most power.

Strategies

Underlining or highlighting the words you feel are significant can be very revealing. If there are more words underlined than not, this is a sure sign of overstressing. Ideas must be seen in their *relative* strength. Though the playwright carefully selects all the words and the actor desires every one to be heard, the audience needs to have them sorted out and prioritized. The musician is trained to do this—he uses dynamics to guide the listener through the melody of his lines. Too many notes at the same level and attack become a blur of noise. The actor must trust that letting some words be unstressed is necessary; they are made clear in relation to other emphasized words.

In natural conversation we often "throw away" some words or let them spill out spontaneously. Working with your scene partner, start each line by saying "of course you know this," then casually toss off the scripted sentence. Notice how this affects your dialogue. Together with your scene partner, identify which lines worked well when said in a casual manner and which did not. Next try punching some words and deemphasizing others. Play with the possibilities. Work to get the idea across to the listener. If you think the *idea* of what you are saying rather than thinking each individual word, your instincts will guide you to which words hold more weight. The average line needs only two or three stressed words; lengthy sentences usually require more. Through careful analysis of the text and experimentation with emphasis, you can determine which words carry the central meaning and power of a line. It can be dangerous, however, to get tangled up in rules, trying to remember how many words to emphasize and how many to throw away. Once you get a feel for the rhythm of the language and the ideas behind what you are saying, the stress falls into place naturally.

When you are unclear about your objective, you may start to listen to yourself and worry about how to say each line. Determine what your character wants to accomplish with these words; why have these specific words been chosen? When directed by a purpose, you will be better able to sense how the words resonate and serve your objective. Certain words will pop out as meaningful and potent, *useful* in getting your point across and having the desired impact on other characters. Drive your energy into those key words and understand that the other words serve to set them up. Analyzing and clarifying will solve many problems.

Additional Thoughts for the Director

If an actor regularly overstresses words, begin by talking about the overall meaning of the lines rather than by trying to fix the emphasis of individual words. Focus on the relevant ideas or themes in a sequence of lines, and work with the actor to select the words that drive the theme. Also remind actors to really listen to one another and to let what they hear affect their responses.

Other Notes of Interest

Emphasize key words.

> My pet peeve is pronouns. For some reason as part of American speech we overemphasize pronouns. These are often givens in the text and hardly need to be lifted at all. It is a weak choice using '*I* like this' '*You* don't do this.' There are countless other options that are much more interesting and reveal more about character. It's demeaning to the character to do that.
>
> —D. Scott Glasser

■ Note

Clean up your diction.

The Problem

The actor's speech is, at times, unintelligible and difficult to follow.

Explanation

When we are children first learning how to speak, we take a great deal of time and effort to discover how our articulators function. In understanding new words, we also are learning how to form them. As we grow older, this information becomes second nature. Rather than concentrating on "how" we are saying things, we focus more on what we are saying.

We have become a visual society. At its beginnings, the theatre was primarily an auditory experience. It was about the spoken word. Nowadays we rely on the visual as much as the aural in the theatre. A beautiful picture *can* speak a thousand words. Because of this, some actors place less importance on their diction. A good play needs to be heard as well as seen. Language and dialogue are essential to the telling of a good story. Every playwright has a unique voice and uses words in a unique way. Every word in a sentence adds up to the overall meaning, and when the audience misses just one word, an entire phrase can be lost. Think about how difficult it is to follow someone who is new to English and is struggling with the language. It takes a great deal of effort on the part of the listener to decipher ideas when some of the speaker's words and phrases are unintelligible.

Clearly, our society has become lazy with words. Many Americans tend to mumble in conversational speech. They fail to open their mouths, move their jaws, and they drop energy at the end of a sentence. Yet when we truly want something, we find the energy and clarity necessary to articulate that desire to the person who can give it to us. Young children can always be heard when it comes to buying that toy for them at the store. The success of a political candidate is as much about the clear articulation of ideas as about the way the ideas are articulated. If you are a good speaker, you have a much better chance of being understood and succeeding in your goals.

Strategies

If you are having difficulty with intelligibility, first go back to your script and circle the nouns and verbs in the lines you have been told are difficult to understand. Practice forming the words in your mouth. Where is the word articulated in your mouth? At the lips? The tip of the teeth? The hard palate or soft palate? Do the words have final consonants that you are losing? Once you have done this, put the words back into the context of the line. Try to make a connection between the word and its modifiers. Are there words you are slurring into other words? Finally, put the sentence in the context of the entire scene.

What words are repeated from line to line? How is that particular choice of word necessary to the scene making sense to the audience?

As always, a good warm-up helps to get your lips, teeth, and tongue moving, especially one that includes difficult tongue twisters. If you always use the same series of exercises to warm up the articulators, your mouth may be getting too used to them. Try varying your routine. Ask other cast members to bring in their favorite exercises to share.

If you are having continual trouble, try slowing everything down. Focus on what you are trying to communicate and why it is important. Remember your speech is key in connecting with your scene partner. Don't take it for granted that you are understandable; make sure your scene partner is hearing and comprehending what you are saying.

Additional Thoughts for the Director

Remind actors that the definition of "diction" relates both to word choice as well as to enunciation. In other words, diction is as much about *what* is being said as about *how* it is being said. Be clear with the actors about what specific words are difficult to comprehend, and clarify for them how these words fit into the overall meaning of the lines. Overenunciation can also be a by-product of this note; the actor may wind up overstressing or hitting words too hard, thus causing the meaning to be lost.

Other Notes of Interest:

Don't rush.

Include the audience.

I find when you tell an actor you need better diction it's just not as helpful, remotely, as using specifics. Either, 'Your character is somebody who is more careful with his speech and this is why . . . ,' or literally, 'These are the three words I'm missing because you're rushing that phrase so much.' Specifics help a lot more.

—Bill Rauch

There's so much lazy speech. Well, I guess that's called naturalism. There are people, and I don't hold it against them, who still want to sound like Marlon Brando. Which only works for Marlon Brando.

—André De Shields

Physical Clarity

◼ Note

Make the blocking your own.

The blocking looks unmotivated.

The Problem

The actor's movements do not look spontaneous or natural to the character.

Explanation

Just as the actor's dialogue needs to appear motivated and spoken for the first time, so does her movement. When an actor is believable, her words and moves seem spontaneous, coming directly from the impulses of her character. If an actor is uncomfortable with a bit of business or a particular cross, the audience senses this. If she has not found a reason behind each move, other than "that's my blocking," her movement will look forced and contrived.

An actor may be faced with many movement challenges, from the simple (a handshake or a walk across the stage) to the more complex (a fight scene, a kiss, or a period mannerism). She may have to navigate an intricate set with multiple stairs, doors, or platforms. She may have blocking dictated to her by the director, or she may be able to improvise her own blocking. Whatever the situation, the actor's job is to look comfortable and natural with her movement and make it seem logical to the character.

This can take time. When we learn a sport, we spend countless hours repeating movements until they become second nature to us. We work on their form and flow and try to perform them with grace and ease. Perfecting blocking usually does not receive as much attention. Actors spend outside rehearsal time running lines but commonly do so while sitting down. Taking time to work physically, rather than just rehearsing in your head, can certainly enhance a performance.

Strategies

If you have a piece of blocking that feels unmotivated, look for the psychological reason behind it. What is going on inside your character at that moment, and how can your move help to express it? How can you connect your character's action and/or emotions to your physicality? Link each move to a thought. For instance, if you have to walk over to a table, identify the impetus behind the move. Perhaps you have just hatched a plan and your physical response is to move forward. Or you are debating ideas and you use the cross to sort through the possibilities. Let every movement spring from what your character is thinking and experiencing.

When you feel awkward or self-conscious in your movement, give yourself time to experiment and work out the details. Go through your blocking and stop anytime a moment does not ring true to you. Repeat it several times varying its timing and pace. You might start a movement earlier or later, pause halfway through it, speed it up, or slow it down. Try a change in posture, a head turn, or gesture. Improvise and see what ideas you can come up with. Look for what the movement needs to clarify your action and have it make sense to you. Once you've discovered which physical nuances work for you, integrate them into your performance creating a physical "score."

Include movement in your personal rehearsal time, as you practice on your own at home. Get up on your feet during the earliest stages of your work, as you are becoming familiar with your lines and starting to memorize them. This way you will establish a strong connection between the physical and psychological aspects of your character. This will serve you well as you link your impulses and motivations to your movement. Once you start to polish your lines, continue to rehearse using your actual blocking. By regularly incorporating movement into your outside rehearsals, you will increase the likelihood of achieving a physically integrated performance.

Additional Thoughts for the Director

Especially with less experienced actors, it is best to get everyone up on their feet early in the process. You want to, as Shakespeare says through Hamlet, "Suit the action to the word, the word to the action" so the actors are continually engaged with not only the words but also how those words are expressed physically.

Blocking can be thought of as a series of advances and retreats between characters. Spend some time with the actors determining where the physical shifts occur in the action. When does a character want to be close to or far from another character? What kind of tension and energy exists between characters? How does the status of the character affect her movement? Relating to the psychology behind the movements can help actors motivate their blocking.

Don't be afraid to abandon blocking that is not working. It is also helpful to assess if actors are comfortable with their movement and, if not, to solicit their suggestions and ideas for improvement.

Other Notes of Interest

Take control.

> You want to work with the director to make sure the movement does not look arbitrary, like 'I'm walking over here only because I've got to pick this chair up.' You want to make the movement part of the character's life, connected to what is going on inside of you.
>
> —Karen Ziemba

■ Note

> Open up physically.
>
> Cheat out.

The Problem

The actors are not opening themselves up to the audience.

Explanation

When we engage in conversations in our everyday lives, it is polite and natural to face the person to whom we are talking. But what feels natural in real life does not always transfer well to the stage. A common habit of beginning actors is to work in profile or to turn their backs to the audience altogether. Experiencing a bit of nervousness or self-consciousness, they feel safer and less "exposed" when they exclude the audience from their view. This position is, of course, less than ideal since the audience misses the actors' expressions and reactions. It is also harder to hear actors when their voices are projected upstage and their lip movements cannot easily be seen. Experienced actors fall victim to this common problem as well. Actors may lose awareness of their stage positions when dealing with a complicated sequence of lines or an intense scene. When two characters are engaged in an intimate conversation, the actors may end up playing the entire scene toward each other in profile. There may be times that having a back to the audience is dramatically effective, and the director may want to use this position. However, for the typical moments, when actors are engaged in dialogue, it is desirable to have them clearly visible.

Strategies

"Cheating out" is a simple technical adjustment that becomes second nature for most actors. Reminding yourself to cheat out whenever possible is a good rule of thumb. To do this, place your downstage foot *slightly* below your upstage foot at about a forty-five-degree angle. If you are angled away from the front of the stage, this small repositioning of your feet opens your torso to the audience, making it easier for them to see your face. Cheating out does not mean you need to face forward; you can be at an angle and still be quite visible.

This position should feel comfortable and natural to you. If you feel awkward, experiment with the placement and angles of both feet. Practice by walking around the stage and stopping in various places. Make whatever small adjustments you need in order to be open to the audience. As you are in rehearsal, periodically ask yourself if you can be seen and remind yourself to cheat out.

Additional Thoughts for the Director

This problem can be addressed to the entire company during a note session. Remind the actors that the play needs to be seen and heard by every member of the audience. When they close themselves off, the action becomes more difficult to follow. If you are playing in a proscenium theatre, the problem is more easily solved. When working in a thrust or arena space, the actors need to pay close attention to where they are facing and at what specific moments in the play they need to open up to the various sections of the audience.

Other Notes of Interest

Include the audience.

Moving into the theatre.

I have to give this note a lot with non-professional actors, early in the process. It helps when people sit in the audience and watch each other. They start learning the power of seeing an actor's face.

—Bill Rauch

Open up physically to the audience, but don't make that apparent to them. Also, don't over cheat. When you're on a thrust stage you don't have to cheat at all. Let the blocking reveal you to the audience. It drives me crazy to see feet facing the audience and head facing the action. Use backs, sides, profiles, voices, the entire body to express on all stages.

—D. Scott Glasser

■ Note

Give focus/take focus.

Find your place in the stage picture.

You are stealing focus.

The Problem

The actor is either taking focus at an inappropriate moment or neglecting to take focus when needed.

Explanation

Theatre is a collaborative art form. It is about artists coming together, joining forces on a single project, and working for the good of the whole. Teamwork is the key, and its importance is especially great for actors. Acting is a delicate balance of give and take between players—one actor passes the baton to the next for the story to be told. Actors must concentrate on fulfilling the requirements of their own roles, while maintaining an awareness of how their parts fit into the bigger picture.

At any given moment in a play, there are usually a small number of characters who are in "focus"; their action is primary and moves the play forward. The attention of the audience should be guided to these characters by careful staging of the director and by participation of all the actors on stage. This way the audience knows where to look to make sense of the action and follow the story. The balance is upset when actors take or give focus indiscriminately.

For instance, we are watching a conflict develop between two people surrounded by a number of citizens out in the town square. The citizens provide a rich texture of reactions to the event. The audience focuses on the conflict and perceives the citizens as a collective response framing the action. If one citizen draws attention to herself (i.e., makes a big move or has a bold reaction at a crucial point in the conflict), we will be distracted from the central action by looking at the wrong place, thus missing dialogue or information essential to the plot. However, if one of the key players fades into the background or does not share her expressions and reactions, we may not notice her and the conflict will not be as effective.

Actors need to develop an awareness of the play as a whole to determine when it is appropriate for their character to take focus and when it is necessary to give focus to others. This ability comes with experience and practice. Some highly animated actors have trouble toning down their energy. For them, taking focus is a habitual, though usually unintentional practice, while giving focus is an uphill struggle. For those who enjoy the spotlight and the approval of the audience, or perhaps distrust their fellow actors, relinquishing focus may not come easily. Conversely, some actors are timid and hesitant to take focus even when it belongs to them. Actors are the most effective at their job when they collaborate. It is in their own best interest, as well as in the interest of the play as a whole, to learn to give and take focus effectively.

Strategies

Many times focus problems develop when you have no dialogue or only intermittent dialogue. When your character speaks, you naturally get the attention of the audience, though it is possible for one actor to overwhelm the stage and take all the focus even when another character is speaking. Let's say you are silent and your reactions are critical to the story, but we are not looking at you because you have not taken our focus. Or you *are* taking focus when we need to be looking elsewhere. In either case, we have been distracted from the central action. To know whether you need to be in focus, assess your character's relative importance to the other characters on stage. This balance will change throughout the play, depending on what is happening at any given moment. Consider the following:

- Is this moment about your character's story?
- Are your reactions crucial to the action?
- Does the audience need to watch you to follow what is going on?

If so, you need to be in focus. A strong stage presence and open physicality are key components. Taking focus can be done by catching the audience's eye through movement, for example, with a gesture, a cross, or a shift in stance. Sometimes a bold move is necessary, other times a turn of the head or a small adjustment of posture may be all that is needed. You and your director may decide you should move to a stronger position on stage. This depends greatly on the configuration of other players; common choices are moving away from a group or moving closer to center stage or downstage, though there are many other possibilities.

If you are not central to the action of the moment, your role is still significant. You help to frame the scene, direct the audience's attention, and provide dimension to the action. Every character is important and should be listening, reacting, and playing the moment. The audience's eye moves from actor to actor, and therefore you can never assume that you are not being watched. Giving focus does not mean you play your character any less fully, but rather you modify and tone down your responses to balance the whole picture. To give focus you can:

- Look at the character(s) who are active, unless your character is meant to ignore the action. This signals the audience to look there as well.

- Place yourself in a secondary stage position (this depends on the placement of other actors and should be decided in concert with the director)—possibilities include placing yourself turned toward, below, or behind the central character(s) or placing yourself in a group off to the side.

- Time your reactions relative to what is happening on stage. You do not want to pull attention away from the main action at inappropriate moments. Be sensitive to when all eyes need to be on the central characters and to when a noticeable reaction from you would be effective.

Be judicious in selecting movements and gestures. Because movement attracts the eye, excessive stage business can easily steal focus. Sometimes making a slight shift in position or even remaining still can be effective choices for the stage picture.

Additional Thoughts for the Director

Step back from a scene and concentrate solely on what you see, letting what you hear fade in importance. Forget what you know about the central action and look for what catches your eye. What gestures, expressions, reactions, or movements draw your attention? Who is most interesting to watch on stage? Is your focus where it should be? Especially when working on a crowd scene, it is key to take time to look at every corner of the stage. Often, actors in large groups will not have a sense of how their movements add to or distract from the full picture. As director, you have the best vantage point and can guide and orchestrate the movement to enhance the story.

Other Notes of Interest

Give your character more status.

Open up physically.

Giving focus and taking focus...if you've been clued in to what the play is thematically, then you'll find that organically.

—Linda Purl

■ Note

Find economy.

You are moving too much.

You are using your body to punctuate each line.

Find stillness.

Simplify.

The Problem

The actor is using too much movement, which is distracting from the performance.

Explanation

It is hard to convince some actors that "less is more." With all eyes of the audience focused on them, actors quickly feel exposed and under pressure to entertain. Anxious to make every moment interesting to watch, actors will push their energy too hard and end up continuously moving. Therefore, each phrase they speak is accompanied by a gesture, each thought is linked with an adjustment of position, and each reaction comes with a turn of the head. Even a second of stillness may seem uncomfortable to them because they are afraid they are not "doing" enough and the moment is not being filled. They become restless and channel their energies into movement. "Surely if I stay in motion," they think, "I will avoid boring the audience."

However, extra effort usually does not pay off. Constant movement becomes a clutter of motion that the audience is unable to process. Because a large number of movements dilute the effectiveness of any single one, no gestures can be especially powerful. Frequently the audience perceives an actor who uses too much movement as nervous. His efforts distract from the physical life of the character, rather than enhancing it. This can divert the audience's attention away from the text. An actor who uses economy in his movement, who selects only the strongest and most expressive moves, will create the clearest characterization.

Strategies

It is always a good practice to take time before rehearsal to do some focused relaxation and breathing exercises. The more you are thinking "in your body," the better chance you will have at being connected to your physical impulses. Work toward centering your drives and emotions deep in your body.

If you find yourself using too much movement, try experimenting with the extremes. Run through a scene adding as much physicality as possible. Gesture on every word, cross the stage at every opportunity, and shift your position constantly. Get your torso, neck, and shoulders involved, as well as your limbs. Follow your every impulse and imbue the scene with physical energy. Note how it felt. Were there moments when the movement seemed unnecessary or excessive? Were there moments when the movement seemed exactly appropriate? Then run the scene again without any movement at all, sitting or standing in stillness. Pin your hands down if necessary to keep them from participating. Avoid using extra head movement to compensate for your lack of gestures. Try not to let the emotional energy of the scene drop during this experiment. Then review your impressions. When did the stillness feel effective? When did you feel a strong need to accentuate a point through gesture? Then run the scene again, this time moving only when it is absolutely necessary—only during those moments when you feel compelled to do so. You will begin to sense which points in the script are best served with movement and which are not.

Gestures need time to be absorbed by the audience. Make a strong gesture, let it live for a moment, and then let its memory linger in the pause. By surrounding gestures with stillness, you give them more potency. Stillness is not emptiness; there can be much life and dynamism in a still moment. Your breath and emotional energy keep you moving on an inner level. Look for the movement in your thought and in your heart—get the other characters to *listen* to you rather than to merely look at you. Concentrate on what is happening internally without giving into the need to externalize each idea.

A common trap is trying to illustrate everything you say with gesture. Avoid the clichés such as indicating yourself when you say "my" or "I," or pointing at others on "you," "she," or "they." Also avoid drawing words or concepts in the air, such as pointing at tears down your face when you talk about crying or miming a book in your hands when you talk about reading. Let the words speak for themselves; your audience will grasp your ideas without seeing them physically illustrated.

Additional Thoughts for the Director

You may immediately recognize an actor's excessive movements as stemming from an urge to look interesting. In this case, you can follow some of the previously described strategies to encourage relaxation and stillness. You also can point out to the actor which of his moments are especially effective and get him to see how they are undermined or blurred by distracting movement. This may help the actor to understand how stillness is actually a positive choice, contributing to a moment rather than experiencing stillness as restraining or holding back energy.

Sometimes other symptoms may surface. Since excessive movements are not integral to the character, they may appear awkward or mechanical. The desire to be constantly entertaining may manifest as tense or forced movements. The actor may not commit fully to a gesture and drop it halfway through. Or the actor may thrust his chin out as he speaks and moves, in an effort to push his energy forward. Look for signs of physical discomfort.

Other Notes of Interest

You are working too hard.

■ Note

> Loosen up.
> Release the tension.

The Problem

The actor is excessively tense on stage.

Explanation

Releasing tension is a common problem in our everyday lives. From driving to work in the morning to trying frantically to accomplish all we need to do in a single day, our tensions build. We start to feel over-worked or misunderstood. Our shoulders tighten, our necks get stiff, and our knees and jaws become locked. Holding unnecessary tension can become habitual. Without knowing it, our bodies become used to the tightness, and we deal with it by ignoring it.

Actors are just as susceptible to tension as anyone; however, if they carry their tension onto the stage, their performance suffers. Actors aim to be free and available conduits for the feelings and emotions of their characters. This can be a challenge, especially when assigned to play tense roles. One of the paradoxes actors face is needing to be free of excess tension while playing tense scenes.

Often, an actor will think she is effective in a scene because she is concentrating intensely and putting a great deal of effort into the moment. But what may be happening is she is substituting tension for energy. Tension can also be a result of overintellectualizing. In this instance, the actor may understand the moment intellectually and work to push its meaning forward, arguing that this extra push helps to communicate her ideas more clearly. She may not even recognize that she is carrying tension. Conversely, when the actor is too laid back, it can look as though she does not care about anything or anyone. She appears lethargic and behaves apathetically. Being either too loose or too tight is unproductive to our lives and ineffective for the stage performer; finding the balance is key.

Strategies

When we are excited about something, but can't seem to make our point clear to another person, the usual advice we receive is to slow down and take a deep breath. Try this just before rehearsing a scene; find a moment to center yourself and take several full breaths. This can release your muscles, relax your body, drop your voice a few pitches, and help to focus your thoughts.

Another key to releasing tension is to concentrate on your alignment. This exercise can be especially useful when you know you are about to play that climactic or intensely emotional moment. Start by stretching out the muscles in your back and neck. As you work through the scene, try to think about lengthening the vertebrae in your neck and spine. Imagine small pockets of air filling the space in between each vertebra. Allow the top of your head to float up as you release the bottom of the spine into the floor. As the tension in the situation increases, increase your awareness of your spine and continue to lengthen as you build to the climactic moment.

We become so serious about our work that we often forget to have fun. A good test as to whether you are having fun with your work can be measured in how you feel after a particularly difficult moment in the play. Do you come off the stage tense and unfocused, or do you feel a sense of release and relaxation, ready to go on to the next scene? Do you feel good about what you did, or are you worried about whether it was successful?

Additional Thoughts for the Director

You want to be careful not to say something that will make an actor become more, rather than less, tense. It helps to give your tension notes about specific moments rather than as a general comment. General comments tend to overwhelm an actor. As you run through a particularly tension-ridden scene, try side coaching the actor, using phrases that combine thoughts about tension and release; for example: "Breathe. Now faster," or "Ease up, keep driving your point." Think about how a doctor delivers a baby—"that's right...breathe...now push...breathe...push, almost there...yes, you've done it."

Other Notes of Interest

Don't rush.

You are working too hard.

■ Note

Control your physical choices.

You are out of control physically.

Be aware of your space.

The Problem

The actor's movements are unpredictable, dangerous, or unrestrained. They are governed by unchecked spontaneity rather than by conscious choice.

Explanation

When actors become physically "out of control," accidents can occur. We have all seen doors slammed too hard or tables kicked in the heat of an impassioned acting moment. Doors, walls, furniture, and props not designed for heavy use are easily damaged, sending technical crews into frenzies. Scenes requiring physical contact can also result in mishap when actors do not exercise caution. Bruises and pain are as possible from a simple arm grab as from a sword fight. A less dramatic, but equally disastrous consequence from an actor's lack of control is a loss of trust from fellow actors. When someone is unpredictable, he becomes an obstacle to the other actors rather than a part of the team. This behavior is rarely intentional or malicious; rather, it indicates a lack of awareness.

Actors who are told they have lost control frequently do not recognize the problem. They feel energized on stage. Fueled by the emotion of the moment, they judge their movements to be honest and connected. Their perception of a strong characterization and a powerful performance may be closely linked to their ability to act immediately from their unmonitored impulses. After all, spontaneity is a desirable quality in a performer.

Acting, however, has boundaries. It is the art of illusion, and actors are trained in techniques that allow them to free their emotions and bodies within a *controlled* environment, controlled being the key word. Actors work together to establish a common set of rules and expectations, so a slap that looks brutal is perfectly safe, or a pounding of a table that sounds destructive is actually quite tame. While a story may call for a character to become physically dangerous and unpredictable, the actor playing the character *never* is. The actor's job is to create the illusion of spontaneity without ever losing the ability to make responsible choices.

Strategies

Take time to physically warm up and work toward establishing a strong sense of grounding. Where are your feet placed? Where is your center of gravity? How is your alignment? Then move to an awareness of what is around you. Where are you in relation to other players, to furniture, to the set? Spend some time alone walking the stage, out of character, examining the playing space. Look at the floor, the walls, the props, etc. Are they sturdy or fragile? Can you find weak points or seams? Talk to the set, costume, and prop designers. Ask if they have any instructions or warnings to give you about how to use items on stage. A wonderful strategy is to spend some time in the shops constructing or watching others construct your show. This is a fast way to appreciate the amount of time and effort that goes into a design as well as to give you an idea of the work that will have to be repeated if something is destroyed by an actor.

When the scene is being staged, communication with scene partners, directors, and choreographers is critical. If you are uncomfortable with a movement for any reason, discuss your concerns with the people involved. Frequently changes can be made or suggestions given that will solve your problems. Likewise, stay in constant communication with other actors to hear their concerns. Take the initiative to ask their opinions; do not assume if your partners are silent no problem exists. Ask: "Am I hurting you? Am I grabbing too hard? Are you comfortable with the movement?" Keep checking with scene partners throughout the rehearsal and performance process to make sure everyone is happy.

Scenes involving simulated harsh physical contact should always be supervised by the fight choreographer and/or the director. Following all guidelines and instructions they provide is absolutely necessary; never improvise with a choreographed combat routine. Regularly begin a rehearsal or performance by running through the sequence of physical movements with scene partners at half the usual speed; this is an essential routine in maintaining safety. Pay attention to the placement of your body, to the exact order and rhythm of movements, and to the partners or properties you are working with. Do not let character or emotion color this purely technical rehearsal. You want to train yourself to keep this technical awareness, especially during performance.

If you feel you are not able to put the same energy into a movement when you are under control, try to channel the energy elsewhere. If you were able to bring power into a moment by slamming your fist onto a desk, but the desk can only support a minimal hit, pull back on your slam and you will still create a believable sound. If you need to grab someone by the shoulder but you are in danger of bruising him, put the muscular tension in your upper arms rather than in your hands where you squeeze. Your body will feel the force while still maintaining the necessary control. If people trained in stage combat are available to you, ask them to watch your movements and make suggestions.

Another excellent place to channel your energy is into your concentration. Make intense character moments a time to intensify your focus on what you are doing. Rather than allowing an emotional rush to guide your stage behavior, let a heightened sense of concentration take the lead. Directing your adrenaline in this way will help you to make safer physical choices.

Additional Thoughts for the Director

To help the actor control physical choices, make sure you leave enough time in the rehearsal process to repeat particularly difficult physical passages. Also check to make sure the actors are making the appropriate eye contact necessary for safety. Remind them that if the actor, not the character, appears to be either in danger or out of control, the audience may find this disturbing and consequently be taken out of the world of the play. If a moment appears to look dangerous, ask each actor privately whether they are in control of the movements, to make sure no one is being hurt. Actors should be absolutely in control of their own safety, and if there is any doubt about this, restage the sequence.

Other Notes of Interest

Connect with your scene partner.

You are working too hard.

Your physical choices, if they're out of control, it just means they're not being connected. They're not truthful.

—Scott Ellis

Commitment

■ Note

You are holding back emotionally.

Let the emotion have more size and power.

The Problem

The actor is underplaying a scene that demands a large emotional commitment.

Explanation

There are a number of roles in the theatre that call for large, fully released emotions. Rage, joy, terror, deep pain, and other raw emotions appear regularly in classic plays, especially in the tragedies of Shakespeare and of ancient Greece. Though not as frequent, these powerful moments also can be found in contemporary plays. Most actors will be faced with the challenge of creating large, pure emotions at some point in their careers.

In our daily lives, we are rarely pushed to the point where we express extreme emotions. More often we suppress or conceal what we are feeling in order to behave by socially appropriate standards. We have much more experience in restraining and holding back than we do in releasing our feelings. We have learned to fight back tears when we are hurt and to bite our lips when we are angry. These reactions have become deeply ingrained habits. It is natural, therefore, when confronted with a role that demands big emotions to feel a little awkward and hesitant. Emotions on this scale seem foreign and exaggerated, not familiar as the naturalism we are used to on stage. When faced with this kind of emotional challenge, it becomes necessary to develop a new sense of honesty and connection to these larger emotional moments.

There are two common reasons that an actor may have trouble reaching emotional peaks. The first is the actor may be afraid to "overdo" and therefore keeps the emotion small and subtle. She may not understand that the character needs to express herself in a heightened manner; consequently, the actor has difficulty finding the motivation and permission to do so. In this case, the actor consciously holds back because she fears appearing forced or unbelievable.

The second reason may be that the actor generates an intense emotion but is not releasing it. The emotion is played on an internal level and is not being shared with others. The actor may feel a powerful connection to what she is saying and experiencing because the sensations are close and personal. But since all of her energy is going inward, none of it reaches the audience. The emotion is not freely unleashed, rather it is being held onto tightly, in an attempt to keep the feeling real and profound. Tension, both physical and vocal, often results from the effort the actor expends on clutching and reeling in the emotion. The actor may tighten her jaw, stomach, or fists, or grip with her throat muscles. Because the emotion is not free and the actor cannot respond easily to the circumstances of the scene, a "psychological tension" can also appear. Some actors let emotion out, then pull it back or bite it off at the end of sentences or thoughts. This emotional pullback prevents emotions from being fully expressed or realized and is another symptom of playing feelings on a too personal level.

Strategies

In general, actors are advised not to concentrate on creating emotions on stage. This can result in indulgent acting, where the actor gets wrapped up in the emotion and loses focus on the action in the scene. Rather, actors need to place themselves in the given circumstances and play concrete actions and let the emotions grow from what they are doing. In plays with heightened emotions, it is important to start with the situation before the emotion. Take time to understand what stakes are involved for the character and why the character has a strong need for emotional release. What are her struggles, challenges, and problems? Understand what the character feels and why this moment is significant for her. This basic work will help you to justify the large emotional commitment.

If you find that you have a difficult time connecting to a strong, larger-than-normal-life emotion, allow yourself to go overboard for awhile. Let each feeling be expressed in a broad physical manner. Speak your lines and accompany them with movements such as throwing objects (pillows or soft balls), swinging your arms, jumping on mats, running around the room—whatever your impulses dictate and safety allows. Use as much of the room as you can and fill it vocally with your words. Imagine your voice is crossing the Grand Canyon and is echoing about. Continue to do this until you have fully committed yourself; when you finish, your heart will be pounding and you may need to catch your breath. When you engage your muscles and breath and commit yourself physically to express an idea, your emotions can more easily find a way out of your body.

If you have an intense connection to the character's feelings, but are not freely releasing them, ask two actors not in the scene to hold you in place as you speak to your scene partner. Either they can stand behind you and hold onto your arms and shoulders or onto the sides of your waist, or they can lean into your chest from the front. As you deliver your lines, have the two actors hold you back as you try to go toward the character you are speaking to. Let the physical energy you expend translate into emotional energy. Work to physically push forward and to express yourself; you will find that your emotions rush out of you with your increased effort. The aim is not to struggle and strain but to open the valve on your emotions and find the physical and mental commitment to what you are saying and feeling. Because you must overcome a physical obstacle in this exercise, it often helps if you eliminate the internal barriers you have placed on yourself.

A less physical method is to have your scene partners walk away when they judge your emotions to be held back. You must make a stronger commitment each time they turn away. This can help you to sense when you are holding back and to judge which parts of the scene are most troubling for you.

Additional Thoughts for the Director

A useful technique for an actor who holds back emotionally is to provide her with the necessary space to make her emotions larger. For the moment in question, put the actor and her partner farther away from each other, so her need to communicate travels a longer distance and consequently carries more intensity.

Try to encourage the actor to make public what she has been feeling too privately or internally. Ask her to envision invading the personal territory of the other character in the scene. Coach the actor to use her words aggressively, using verbs such as "to hurt" or "to attack"; this puts the actor in control and helps protect her from feeling too vulnerable.

Other Notes of Interest

Give your character more status.

Take a risk.

Raise the stakes.

Concentrate on the action, not the emotion.

If you're holding back, it's probably because you don't feel safe, and for a director to tell you you're holding back can feel like an attack. So now he/she has moved you five paces further away from where you want to be. If you're with a director you've worked with a long time, and there's a great deal of trust and understanding, maybe this could work. A better way of getting the same idea across is 'take a risk.' It's about giving someone permission, creating a safe place in which an actor can take chances.

—Linda Purl

■ Note

Take a risk.

That choice is too easy.

Give yourself permission.

The Problem

The actor is avoiding more challenging or difficult experimentation by sticking to choices that are easy to play.

Explanation

Learning to take risks is part of all actor training. From placing their trust in fellow actors, to being in front of an audience, actors continually face emotional risks, putting themselves in positions where they are exposed and vulnerable. Creative risks are demanded in the rehearsal process, as actors build characters and shape performances. Developing new skills and expanding range may cause actors to confront psychological risks.

Though an actor frequently may be asked to take risks, this does not mean the process ever becomes easy; in fact, it may *always* be a serious challenge. Risks require bravery, emotional strength, and a great deal of energy. And every risk carries with it the possibility of failure. We all fear looking stupid, of making a fool of ourselves, and in the theatre we risk doing so in front of large numbers of people. It is natural to try to protect ourselves from embarrassment and shy away from major risks.

An actor avoids risks by finding a safe approach, something along the lines of "the path of least resistance." For instance, an actor may develop a role and find a logical characterization, make some straightforward choices early in the rehearsal period, and stick with those choices without further exploration. While the basic requirements of the role may be fulfilled—there is nothing wrong with the performance—it is predictable and lackluster. There are no surprises, no dimension, no excitement. The actor has created the most obvious, noncontroversial interpretation, without ever having to look underneath the surface of the character. No one will say the actor was bad, but then again, no one will be particularly moved or intrigued by her work.

Strategies

Sometimes the biggest risk is admitting to yourself that something is missing in your performance. Answering "yes" to any of the following questions may indicate your performance is too safe:

- Are you enjoying your performance, or just running through the lines?
- Are you bored when you come to a certain point in the play?
- Do scenes lack drive and energy?
- Do you feel yourself holding back?
- Are you frightened by riskier moments? Are you concentrating on your fear rather than on the action?

A key element in successful risk taking is giving yourself permission to fail. If there are people around you taking risks, this makes it easier to feel comfortable doing so yourself. If not, you can take the first risk and inspire others to do the same. Or if you are feeling a little insecure, be direct and ask for the permission: "I'd like to try something new here. Is that all right?" Once you are given the green light, either by someone else or by your own determination, you will feel more open about taking risks at other moments. Remember the rehearsal room is the place to experiment, to go out on a limb, and to fall flat on your face. That is what you are supposed to do; failing is a necessary and expected part of the process. Only by allowing yourself to fail can you ever hope to unearth the great ideas. "Right" and "perfect" are concepts that do not exist in the arts, but we can aspire to being daring and innovative.

If you are shy about plunging in and taking big risks, you can begin by experimenting with the intensity level of the choices you have already made. Say you have a scene in which you are criticizing another character. Gradually increase the degree of intensity of this moment. First play it a bit more harshly, then even more so, then with vicious intent, then allow yourself to go over the top in your attack. Play with the extremes. This may spark some interesting responses in your scene partner and generate some new ideas not apparent at first. Maybe it won't work at all, but you can come back to your original choices with a new commitment and understanding. Once you are comfortable with experimenting in this manner, open yourself to other risks: improvising, playing with opposites, following impulses, trying radical ideas, etc.

Risk taking is a process of discovery and not a means to an instantaneous result. Many of your attempts will yield nothing worthwhile; many ideas will be tried and discarded. In fact, you may feel lost some of the time, without a clue about how you are going to end up playing your role. Stay engaged with the process, and over time you will find the exciting ideas you are hoping for. If you focus on the final product, you will inhibit your creativity and may even convince yourself that the safe choices are the best ones. Certainly they help you to feel secure early in rehearsals, but they will never be as interesting or vibrant as riskier choices.

Additional Thoughts for the Director

Inspirational words can often encourage an actor to experiment and take a chance on a more edgy choice. Often a director will repeat the same thoughts over and over without getting through to the actor. Try discussing the scene from a new angle. By finding a fresh perspective, the actor will be more inclined to risk changing his current choice for something with more depth and variety. Creating a rehearsal environment where actors feel free to explore is important. Be sure to give verbal permission to the actors to experiment on risky choices and applaud both their successes and failures.

Other Notes of Interest

You are setting choices too early.

Follow your impulse.

You are holding back emotionally.

Take a risk...by making choices. Take a risk by making a stronger choice, always. It might work, it might not.

—Scott Ellis

■ Note

You are thinking too much.

Get out of your head.

Avoid overintellectualizing.

The Problem

The actor is relying too heavily on an intellectual understanding of the role, blocking any emotional connection.

Explanation

For many years of our lives we are rewarded for sitting still, thinking hard, and monitoring our actions. The more we develop our intellect, we are told, the better chance we have at success. When asked to abandon a cerebral approach and to act from our heart rather than from our head, we naturally struggle and resist. "Stop thinking? How can I control my performance?" It is understandably difficult to let go of a familiar process and go against what we have been taught. Analytical thinking gives us security and guidance in an art form known for creating insecurity. However, as artists, we are in the business of human passions and instincts. Staying locked in our head distances us from our impulses and prevents us from being emotionally connected to our character. This is not to say intellectual analysis and thoughtful preparation are not essential to the creative process—they are. But there is a time in rehearsal when actors must trust they have done enough thinking and allow themselves to *give in* to the experience of the role.

A sure sign of thinking too much is a persistent urge to explain or justify choices. Actors who stay trapped in their head think their emotions and thoughts are coming across; they have analyzed their role fully and their performance feels right to them. Therefore, they do not believe critiques and easily launch into intellectual discussions of what they have just done. They are adept at using words and arguments to persuade listeners that they lived and felt the character's emotions, even if their audience was unmoved.

Another indication of this problem is manifested physically; the actor is acting only from the neck up. The eyes may sparkle, the face is expressive, and the head moves to accentuate the character's thoughts; however, the rest of the body—especially the torso—remains disengaged. Because the actor is not physically open, she cuts off emotion from being expressed through her body. All of this excess energy gets channeled back upward and becomes head movement.

Strategies

Getting your body to be physically responsive is one means to open your emotional connection. The first step is a thorough warm-up before rehearsal to prepare your body to work. Include limbering and stretching, aerobic exercise, and relaxation as part of your routine. If you find some days you do not have time for a complete warm-up, even a couple of minutes of movement can be extremely helpful. You can also use the time you have while waiting in the wings for some quick stretches; this may have the double benefit of keeping you from "thinking too much" before an entrance.

To help ground yourself physically, select a location in your torso where you will center your character's energy. To identify an appropriate "center," you can ask yourself the following questions:

- Where does your character feel pain?
- From where does your character draw strength?
- Where does your character feel vulnerable?
- Where does your character store emotions?
- Where does your character sense impulses?

The stomach, heart, chest, solar plexus, and pelvis are common choices. Concentrate on your center and imagine your breath running to and from this spot. Experiment walking around the room letting your movement be affected by your choice. During rehearsal, try to "listen" through your body. As the other characters speak, let their words, their praise, their anger enter you at your center. And as you say your lines, let your ideas originate from this place. Root your emotions deep in your torso rather than in your head. This exercise demands imagination and careful focus as well as many hours of practice.

If you are accused of talking too much in rehearsal, use a self-imposed period of silence. Ban yourself from participating in any discussions for an hour, a full rehearsal, or even a week of rehearsals. Listen to and accept what you hear from your director. Try ideas suggested to you without questioning them. Do not worry if you disagree or if you do not understand every idea completely. Let this quiet time help you to get inside your character. At the end of your silence, only discuss your "burning issues"—be selective.

Additional Thoughts for the Director

Actors who overintellectualize in rehearsal have often put a lot of time and thought into their roles. This effort needs to be acknowledged and commended before a note is given. You want to avoid either insulting the work of the actor or causing the actor to shut down. A sensitive actor may interpret a request to hold back her explanations to mean the same as "Shut up!" For such actors, it may be best to discuss this note in private.

Besides working physically with an actor as detailed previously, you can use techniques to shake up a scene and break the patterns of the actor. These techniques require an actor to think quickly, abandon logic, and perform without worrying about being "good." Run the scene and call out a series of varying action verbs. Ask the actor to quickly adjust to new verbs without giving her time to plan or to think about her approach. Pick some verbs in line with the intent of the scene and others that are outrageous or off-the-wall. Coach the actor to follow impulses and to do whatever comes into her mind, regardless of whether it makes sense. Ask the actor to go against her intellectual perception of the scene. Work with opposites. If the scene is serious, play it as a comedy. If the actor has been playing subtleties, ask her to play it big. If the character is gritty, have her play it with a delicate and sensitive touch.

Other Notes of Interest

Follow your impulse.

Take a risk.

You are working too hard.

■ Note

You are monitoring your performance.

You are judging your work when on stage.

The Problem

The actor's concentration is focused on assessing his performance, preventing him from connecting fully with his character.

Explanation

It is common for us to keep a running commentary of our actions inside our heads. Thoughts such as "Why did I say that?", "I feel uncomfortable.", or "I just impressed them!" are typical inner responses a person might have while engaging in a conversation. We like to monitor how we are coming across and observe how we are being judged. We also secretly criticize and applaud our various actions as we do them, either berating ourselves for poor choices or rejoicing with pride for good ones. This "inner monologue" is our way to evaluate what we do and to guide us in making future decisions.

Likewise, actors privately critique their performance as they are performing. Some part of their mind is keeping track of how effective they are and how the audience is responding. Whether it be a full audience or an audience composed of the director and fellow actors, it is important for actors to be able to learn from each performance and to shape and refine their roles based on how choices succeed or fail. The only way to know if an idea will work on the stage is to try it out and appraise the results.

However, an actor can become preoccupied with judging how he is doing and make that his primary focus. He may say a line and think: "How did that sound? Is that how I intended that line? That didn't come out right. Why aren't they laughing?" He listens and watches himself and evaluates how convincing he was. He keeps a running list of which choices seemed to work and which ones need to be discarded. Though this self-critique is usually present on some level, when it becomes the main concern, it can block the actor from connecting to the emotions and drives of his character. The actor is worrying more about *how* he is doing rather than being involved with *what* he is doing. To the audience the actor appears "distanced" from his role because he is thinking *about* his character more than he is thinking *as* his character.

Strategies

If you find your self-monitoring is getting in the way of delivering a compelling performance, you might try using an "inner monologue." Instead of concentrating on what you as the actor are thinking, discover the thoughts that are running through the mind of your character. Just as you judge yourself and what you say, find how your character is judging himself. For instance:

- What options is he weighing in his mind?
- What are his opinions, worries, and secret thoughts?

- When the character speaks, is he inwardly nervous, critical, admiring, or proud?
- Is he self-conscious or planning out what to say?
- Is he pleased or displeased with what is going on?

If you concentrate on what is inside the character's head, this will immediately connect you to what the character feels and wants and help to put you into his shoes. You will become more involved in the action of a scene and will have less time to focus on your own running commentary.

Another technique is to keep an actor's notebook. After you have completed a scene or performance, go to your notebook and log your impressions, ideas, and concerns while your work is still fresh in your mind. By scheduling a habitual time to review and evaluate *after* each performance, you are less likely to be compelled to judge yourself *while* you are performing. The evaluation process continues inside of you, whether you make it your top priority or not. Assess your work only after a performance, and not during, in order to keep your mind clear and focused while acting.

Additional Thoughts for the Director

Be careful how you phrase this note. If the actor appears to be monitoring what he is doing, reassure him that when he is focused on the other character in the scene he is more engaging and interesting to watch than when he appears to be thinking only about himself. Suggest specific ideas as to what the character would be thinking at various moments in the play. By helping the actor organize the character's journey in his mind, you significantly decrease the chance that he will have time to monitor or judge his performance.

Other Notes of Interest

You are thinking too much.

■ Note

Connect with your scene partner.
You are acting alone.
Listen.

The Problem

The actor is having difficulty affecting or being affected by a scene partner.

Explanation

Drama comes from interaction and the changing dynamics between two characters. Chemistry between two actors is a genuine give and take of reaction and response. One character makes a statement and suddenly there is tension in the moment and anticipation about what will happen next. We look to see how that other person will respond, what her expression will be, and what she will spontaneously say or do. The two actors are making a connection as characters.

When an actor is wholly focused on herself, there is a danger that the audience will lose interest. There is no reason to look back and forth between the two actors because there is little exchange of energy passing between them, so the audience gets bored.

Though usually an actor is aware of the importance of interaction, she may become overwhelmed by the role and consequently keep her circle of concentration only around herself. This means she does not react to the impulses, the timing, and the nuances of her fellow actors on stage, nor does she send her own energy out toward others. She relies on her own inner resources, keeps her focus on her own performance, and does not tap into what is happening around her.

Strategies

To connect with your scene partner, you want to give her your full focus. This means taking the time to listen to her, watch her, and sense her presence. To practice this, sit opposite her and make eye contact while you run your scene. Make sure you are really looking at one another and seeing how you both react to specific moments in the text. Be conscious of whether you are glassy-eyed or not (looking but not really seeing) and make conscious decisions as to when you are really *looking* and when you need to *look away.*

Next, run through your lines on your feet without any attempt at "performing." Let go of any previous interpretations you may have made and try to live spontaneously in the moment. Do not plan how you will deliver your lines, what your expression will be, where you will move, or how you will feel about what is happening. When your partner speaks, let yourself be affected by what she is saying and how she says it. React to her spontaneously. Next, watch for how you have affected her by what *you* say and do. Take in her response to your lines. Keep your focus on what is happening in front of you in the present moment and try not to get ahead of yourself.

Additional Thoughts for the Director

If you feel an actor is having difficulty connecting with her scene partner, try having her redefine her objective in terms of the other character. Offer as many tactics as you can think of to help the actor force her will on the other character and pursue her goal. Give specific notes as to when the actor is looking away at an inappropriate moment in the scene and as to when she needs to make specific eye contact with the other character. Use phrases such as "to unmask" or "to penetrate" to make her eye contact specific.

Other Notes of Interest

Follow your impulse.

> I've found a director just reminding me to 'listen' has been one of the most valuable notes. It is the key to so much. It puts you specifically into the scene and it anchors you to its reality. It gives you an action and it takes you out of yourself. It is a magical note. I think when all else fails, a director can always say 'listen.'
>
> —Linda Purl

■ Note

> Include the audience.
> Project.
> It is too personal, too small.
> Play to the balcony; play to the back wall.

The Problem

The acting is too subtle or the actor's volume too soft to reach the audience.

Explanation

In film acting, subtlety is the key. The camera catches and magnifies every move; a slight adjustment of a smile, a lift of an eyebrow or a quick swallow is all that is needed to electrify the screen. Lines are often delivered in a conversational tone, or even whispered, and then enhanced by sophisticated sound technology. For the screen—where the image is huge and the sound speakers surround the room—this approach works beautifully, but for the stage it is far from effective.

Theatre demands an acting style that is larger than life and an energy level that reaches beyond the confines of the stage. There is no camera to amplify expressions or to focus our attention. The actor must do the work himself; he must generate the vocal, physical, and emotional energy needed to reach every member of the audience. The larger the theatre, the farther the energy must be sent. This can feel unnatural and forced at first, especially for actors who equate being subtle with being truthful. However, if performances are inaudible, underplayed, or too small in scale for the size of the theatre, they will be perceived as "flat" and without drive or charisma.

Strategies

Trying to make your performance bigger or "larger than life" will misdirect your energy and lead to self-conscious and insincere acting. A better approach is to think of "sharing" your performance with the audience. Start gradually. First, play a scene concerning yourself just with the other characters on stage. Your volume, gestures, facial expressions, and energy need only be enough to communicate with them. An observer standing a few feet away should not be able to hear or perceive what is happening. Next, play the scene including the first two rows of the theatre. Notice how you adjust: you open yourself physically to be visible, you project your voice a little more, and you become a bit more expressive. Continue this by including half of the audience and then finally the entire house. Have someone sit in the back row of the theatre and project to him, while keeping your connection with the other actors on stage. By expanding your performance gradually, you are better able to maintain a sense of truth in your actions, while sharing them with a larger circle of people.

Another important strategy is to make vocal and physical warm-ups a part of your daily routine. Warm-ups can help to release excess tension and energize you for rehearsal, which in turn makes you more comfortable in using your voice and body boldly. Try to include a wide variety of elements in your warm-up, from breath work, vocalizing, and tongue twisters to stretches and movement exercises.

Additional Thoughts for the Director

Projection notes are perhaps the most common ones given to an actor during the final stages of rehearsal. For a director, it can be a frustrating time; brilliant acting counts for nothing if an audience can't hear what's being said. Addressing volume issues early is the best approach, especially if you are rehearsing in a room smaller than the performance space. Encourage actors to project from the first moments they get on their feet, so they immediately connect vocal energy with portraying their character. Once actors get used to small voices and subtle choices, it is much harder for them to play it bigger and still feel their acting is honest. However, if you find yourself near performance time still not being able to hear your actors, sit in the back row of the audience and have actors project to you. Ask them to project the *meaning* of their lines rather than just the words. You want to keep the actors' focus on communicating ideas, otherwise they may end up shouting their lines, thus losing any nuance. If more than one actor is having a volume problem, have them come out into the audience and listen to one another. Remind actors to boost their volume if they are blocked to turn upstage or away from the audience. Encourage actors to do their vocal and physical warm-ups on the stage rather than in a small corner backstage. You may want to consider group warm-ups prior to rehearsal; this ensures that everyone does a warm-up and helps to boost the energy of the cast as a whole.

Other Notes of Interest

Drive energy through to the end of the line.

You are holding back emotionally.

Open up physically.

Raise the stakes.

Moving into the theatre.

It has to start small to go big. You have to have a solid foundation before you can send it out there.

—Linda Purl

Instead of saying 'Play to the back of the theatre,' I would say something more like 'Embrace everyone in the theatre.'

—Libby Appel

If you are doing a classical text or moving into a 'barn' of a theatre, the director has got to start early giving those notes. Generally, if it is too intimate then stylistically you have made some wrong choices. Especially in a language play, if you can't hear the language then there is no text, there is no action, there is nothing.

—Boyd Gaines

■ Note

Find the vulnerability.

The Problem

The actor's portrayal of the character lacks a vulnerable side.

Explanation

As an audience member we are privileged; we are invited inside the lives of characters to learn their hopes, fears, faults, and desires. We see beyond just the surface level; we get to see into their humanity. This allows us to learn from them, relate to them, and be moved by them. When this happens, a performance is memorable.

It is up to the actors to bring the humanity of the characters to life. Some characters will be written as sensitive and open; others, as closed and rigid. We may encounter characters who appear to be impervious to attack, incapable of being wounded, or strong willed and defiant. Finding their vulnerability is more of a challenge. But their strength may come from their inability to let others in. They may guard themselves from hurt and from appearing weak. They are on the defensive at every moment and refuse to be exposed or unprotected. They are afraid of feeling or admitting that they can be sensitive and susceptible. Every character, no matter how insecure or how proud, has a vulnerable side. Those moments, when the character drops the walls and lets us see who they really are, are electric on stage.

Strategies

Begin by identifying who or what event in the play is capable of making you feel vulnerable. When does another character "push your buttons" or "get too close"? When are you challenged to change, grow, or self-reflect? Look for moments of tension, crisis, or confrontation when you must face important questions. Is there a place in the action where it is necessary for you to show your vulnerable side; do you have a breaking point?

Vulnerability can manifest itself in many, sometimes opposing ways. More sensitive characters may reveal their vulnerability in immediate and obvious manners, while those with stronger skins may work hard to prevent any weakness from showing. For the latter type of characters, the point when they seem the most confident and are putting up the strongest front is often the point when they are feeling the most insecure. Look beneath the surface and question your behavior. Do you:

- lash out at people? become aggressive?
- retreat into yourself?
- become defensive or overly confident?
- become fearful or insecure?
- admit a secret?
- feel guilt or regret?
- listen to criticism?
- open yourself to love?
- risk rejection?
- become affectionate?
- touch others, but not allow others to touch you?

You may allow yourself to appear vulnerable, letting other characters see you open and unprotected. Or you may fear this state and maintain an outward presentation of strength while inwardly feeling, experiencing, and coping with your true vulnerable self. In either scenario, your character will have more dimension and fascination for the audience.

Additional Thoughts for the Director

Help the actor to clearly identify where in the play the character is most susceptible to her inner feelings. If the actor is continuing to have trouble being open, try discussing her own personal fears about the moment in question. It may be she is holding back, waiting to get in front of an audience. Remind her this kind of work needs to be done in rehearsals, so the vulnerable moments are not left to chance; she will hit these moments in performance after performance only if she is sure of her objective and has a strong action to play.

Other Notes of Interest

Look for the opposite.

You are holding back emotionally.

Take a risk.

Vulnerability is the key to empathy from an audience. Audiences respond to those things in a character that make the character most like the audience. If you are only strong, only winning. If you're only heroic. If you're only larger than life, then you won't be heard. You have to find the Achilles heel. Not everything is tragic, but if there is no soft spot, no soft underbelly, no wound—then there's no identification.

—André De Shields

When you're lost in the vagaries of trying to find a character, something specific in the physicality of the character, or the climate of the room, can anchor you.

—Linda Purl

■ Note

Give your character more status.

Your character needs a stronger presence.

The Problem

The actor is playing a high-status character too timidly.

Explanation

There are characters who, from the moment they enter the stage, have a certain kind of star power. Call it charisma or call it "presence," the energy they emanate is palpable and quickly draws the focus of the other characters. Perhaps admired or perhaps feared, they are the leaders, the heroes, the villains, the memorable personalities. Many characters from historical plays fit into this category: Cleopatra, Julius Caesar, Jesus Christ, Saint Joan, and Elizabeth I are prime examples. Recreating these well-known figures and dealing with their enormous reputations is especially challenging. But there are just as many fictional characters who fit this description: Medea, Mercutio, Merlin, Cyrano de Bergerac, Lady Bracknell, and Dolly Levi are a few such roles. They may or may not have the most time on stage, but whenever these characters appear, their special presence is evident. Filling the shoes of a high-status character can place extraordinary demands on the actor.

Strategies

People who have status and presence don't have to work at it; they just *have* it. So how does an actor, perhaps a bit shy in his own life, embody such a person without showing the effort? Determined to capture the essence of a character, many actors mistakenly focus on the outward appearance of status. They end up playing a general sense of the character's "charisma" rather than playing the person underneath.

To create a specific, believable character, a good first step is to understand what it is about this person that garners the respect of others.

- What are his talents?
- Can he command people's attention?
- How does he think and speak? Is it quickly? Decisively? Methodically?
- What are his opinions, convictions, or aspirations?
- What position does he hold in society or among family and friends?
- Does he have the ability to focus other people's thoughts?
- Does he inspire, astonish, manipulate, intimidate, or threaten others?
- What is it about his past history that impresses his peers?

Develop a thorough biography of your character, examining his background, relationships, and personality traits. Absorb this information and visualize your character and his life. Create a "mental movie" of how he travels through his day. Let this information guide you as you select objectives and actions and make physical and vocal choices.

A powerful character does not always have to command the limelight. This is especially important to remember if you feel your performance is forced. Power is very often manifested in a quiet stillness, a physically grounded presence, or an intense focus. Be sure your work is specific; have a clear, precise, inner monologue and know what your character wants and why. Then experiment with how much you can *let go* of the situation. Try letting events happen around you rather than making great efforts to control them. This does not mean you are apathetic or without energy; no doubt you have great energy, but you do not have to struggle to get what you want. Look for the balance point between working too hard and too little—a place of ease.

Additional Thoughts for the Director

You can help the actor embrace more status by focusing the work of the other actors around him. Have the characters assemble on stage in order of rank and position in society, and then have your high-status character make a grand entrance. As he slowly walks through the assembly greeting everyone, the individual characters make reverence to this person. Before you begin this exercise, have the actors clarify their outward intentions. Whether they like or dislike this character, they still must do him honor. You can also play this exercise in a more spontaneous way. Without telling the actor portraying the high-status character, have all the other actors decide on an action, which when played, will show great respect for their peer. Then play this game subtly throughout an entire rehearsal, ending with a group discussion. These actions do not have to be just about flattery, but can range in depth and complexity, such as to win respect, to inwardly adore, to watch his every move, to keep him at a distance, to seek his wisdom, etc.

Other Notes of Interest

Take the stage.

Take control.

■ Note

Take the stage.

The Problem

The actor lacks the requisite stage presence to fulfill a particularly powerful moment in the play.

Explanation

Most plays have moments that are "electric," those points when you can't take your eyes off the stage. Something crucial is happening in the play and you can feel the energy of the actors drawing you closer into the story. Quite often there is one character who is transforming the action of the play, and it is this character who holds your focus. Maybe she is sharing important news, creating a moment of crisis, or performing an unexpected act of bravery. She could be involved in something hilarious, or maddening, or surprising, even mysterious. This character needs to grab our attention forcefully and command the stage. The actor must have a powerful presence to do so. For instance, in *My Fair Lady*, after her triumph at the Embassy Ball, Eliza Doolittle must, for the first time, confront Professor Higgins about his behavior and her future position. Though she is written as a strong-willed character, rich with large comedic moments, this particular exchange between the two lead characters is a serious moment in the story and demands a great deal of emotional commitment from the actor playing Eliza. Another example can be found in *Macbeth*, when Seyton must enter and inform Macbeth of his wife's fate: "The queen, my lord, is dead." This simple, single line carries with it a profound message. Moments such as these that drive the action forward require a strong stage presence; they cannot afford to be played with timidity.

There can be many obstacles to "taking the stage" successfully. Actors who are shy by nature often have a difficult time asserting themselves without feeling self-conscious. It may take a number of rehearsals and a lot of reassurance before they are able to overcome their discomfort and throw themselves into what they are doing. When faced with smaller roles, even confident actors have trouble creating a strong stage presence, because they have little stage time to build up the needed intensity. An even more challenging task is making only one brief appearance in a play, but having to enter at full power; such is the case with messenger speeches in ancient Greek plays.

Strategies

Establishing a powerful "presence" on stage is a somewhat elusive task. It requires an intense focus, a firm understanding of the action, and a strong physical commitment. When you and your director have identified a moment your character needs to have a strong presence, consider these questions:

- What is your purpose?
- How do you affect the other characters?
- How do you affect the action at that moment?
- How do you change the course of the story overall?
- What is the significance of what you are saying and doing?

Having a clear purpose will help you to focus your energies and to invest fully in your objective. Once you know your intent, you can demand that the other characters listen to what you have to say. Seize their attention; crave to be heard. Assert your energy boldly. Experiment with "overplaying" your moment, taking it to an extreme, and then assess what kind of effect you have on the other characters.

Though your posture and stance will be determined by the traits of your character, you can incorporate some of the following physical suggestions into your portrayal, making any necessary adjustments to stay consistent with your unique circumstances.

- Establish a strong base, feet planted firmly, with a sense of connection to the ground.

- Keep your body open (rather than closing off or protecting yourself).

- Let full breaths drop into your body; breathe from your diaphragm.

- Establish clear eye contact with those you are speaking to (though you do not need to "lock" your focus).

- Release excess tension, focus your energy on communicating and affecting those around you.

When your body is open and grounded, you are able to channel more power as an actor, and therefore have more presence.

Additional Thoughts for the Director

An actor, after hearing this note, may end up pushing too hard, feeling as though everything hinges on her performance. She may focus on the result of a "strong presence" and lose connection with the moment-to-moment thought process of her character. Work first on increasing the actor's commitment to her action (raising the stakes) and on helping her fully understand the importance of her role at that point in the story. Once the actor has a grasp of this, then move to the size of her performance, helping her find the happy medium between being too subtle and too deliberate. Also, by coaching surrounding characters to focus their attention and energy toward this person, you may help the actor find the confidence to take the stage.

Other Notes of Interest

Enter/exit dynamically.

Give focus/take focus.

Raise the stakes.

Give your character more status.

I would never tell someone to 'take the stage' because I'm not sure they would even know what that means. But I would say, 'Listen, you're walking into a room, obviously your choices aren't very strong because I'm not even looking at you.' You know, you've got to come in with strong choices. Make strong choices.

—Scott Ellis

■ Note

Take control.

Own your performance.

Make it your own.

Commit to the action.

The Problem

The actor is doing everything as rehearsed but lacks a full commitment to the role.

Explanation

There is a moment in the rehearsal process when an actor's performance is falling into place—lines are learned and understood, an interpretation is crystallizing, blocking and timing are appropriate—and yet something seems to be missing. We sense the actor is holding back; he has yet to commit fully to his role and consequently the character is not believable. We are still aware we are watching an actor who has memorized and rehearsed his part, and this keeps us from being completely swept away by the illusion of the play. That final magical leap has not been made, when the actor moves from running competently through his role, doing what he has been told to do, to the point where he owns his performance. We are still waiting for the character to come alive.

Initially, an actor has to focus on the many technical aspects of his role. He spends time making decisions about his character, exploring ideas, integrating the director's comments, and learning the mechanics of the part. This work becomes the foundation for later inspiration. Then there comes a point when the actor's focus changes from learning his role to embodying it, when he can trust that his preparation is solid enough to support him. This is similar to a young child taking the training wheels off his bicycle. There is a moment of uncertainty at first, but once the child decides to be daring and pedal ahead with full power and commitment, he discovers how to keep his balance. Then he becomes in control of his bicycle and learns how to guide and maneuver it freely. An actor can find the same sense of confidence and freedom when playing a role.

Strategies

Being in the right frame of mind helps you feel ready to take charge of your performance. Once you are familiar with your role, you can relax and have fun with it. The tough work is done; now is when you can enjoy your time on stage. Focus your energy and throw yourself boldly into what you are doing. Relish your character's secrets, your interesting moments, and your exciting interactions with other characters. Give yourself freedom to explore new nuances and approaches. More than likely, by the end of the rehearsal period, you know your character better than anyone else. Your timing, your delivery, your interpretation are uniquely yours. Let this give you the extra confidence you need to fully commit to your choices.

It is also important to drop yourself fully into the character's world and believe completely in the given circumstances. Reinvest in what the character is committed to. Remind yourself of what passions and drives fuel the character's energy. How can you make the character's passions your own? Find substitutions in your own life that relate to the emotions and objectives of your character. Establish personal connections to the experiences in the play. Make the character's life specific and meaningful to you. In the end, owning a role depends on your willingness to let go of a "by rote" performance and to give yourself over to your character. It is a risk that demands powerful concentration, but the rewards are high.

Additional Thoughts for the Director

Hand in hand with the actor taking control of his performance is the director allowing this to happen. Push the bird out of the nest and let him take wing. You may want to only refer to the actor by his character name during note sessions. In this way, the actor will feel a sense of ownership in regards to his character. You want to make sure that what you have been working on together is now something he respects as his own.

Other Notes of Interest

You are thinking too much.

Follow your impulse.

Depth and Variety

■ Note

Raise the stakes.

Upgrade the objective.

Fight harder for what you want.

The Problem

The moment lacks intensity, energy, and/or commitment from the actor.

Explanation

It is a common mistake for an actor to play a scene too small or too casually for fear of appearing unrealistic. After all, our everyday lives are mostly filled with low-key events that do not demand extraordinary intensity on our part. Our desire to be natural and realistic on stage often leads us to keep our acting equally understated. Even more, the acting style in most television and film is restrained, reinforcing our perception that subdued performances are the most truthful.

Plays, however, are about the heightened moments in characters' lives. Playwrights tend to eliminate the trivial and concentrate on the critical, life-changing events; these events are the most interesting to watch. Every scene is an important first-time experience for the character, even "noncrisis" scenes. Therefore, the actor will need to use more energy and drive than what she is normally accustomed to using. It is necessary for the actor to risk feeling a little unnatural or foolish at first to achieve the intensity which the character requires.

Making the moment important involves picking bolder objectives and actions and committing fully to them. If an objective is not powerful enough, it needs to be made stronger and more important to the character. When an actor is playing an objective, but the scene remains lackluster and flat, it is often because the actor is not driven by desire to achieve her goal. She has not really connected with her partner, she is not making strong choices, and she doesn't appear to really want what she is after.

Strategies

Intensify your objective by picking the strongest words to express what your character wants. Words are powerful tools. If you pick the right ones, they can guide and focus your work as well as inspire you to make new choices. Take time to consider which words truly capture what it is that drives your character. Look for words that energize you. Use a thesaurus and/or dictionary to help you find a variety of possibilities before you decide on one. A weak objective can be "upgraded" to a strong one by substituting a stronger word. For example, if your objective is "to *ask* for forgiveness," try inserting "to *plead*" or "to *demand*" forgiveness. If you are using the phrase "to *displease*," instead try "to *infuriate*." Pick words that suggest bolder acting choices to you.

The given circumstances are also of crucial importance. Examine the scene and find the obstacles that your character faces, those elements that complicate your pursuit of your objective. There may be obvious obstacles—such as a disagreement among characters—but also look beyond the surface for other stumbling blocks. Are there psychological, emotional, physical, or social issues that impede your character? Knowing what you must fight against can give you an extra boost of adrenaline and intensity. You can also use artificial obstacles to heighten the circumstances. Add urgency by setting a time limit, such as "you must accomplish your objective in the next minute" or "your enemy is about to enter at any moment and you must hurry." Or add life-threatening circumstances; in other words, your life depends on you achieving your goal. Establishing a reward may help to motivate you: "If you win your objective you will receive a million dollars." Let your imagination and your character's situation guide you to other ideas. Such given circumstances can be either effectively used as rehearsal techniques or, if they are appropriate to the context of the scene, be incorporated into the performance.

If you need to reevaluate your chosen objective, ask yourself the following questions:

- Is it of critical importance to your character? Is it something your character wants to fight for?
- How is your objective in this scene related to what you are fighting for in the whole play?
- Is your objective focused on what you want from other character(s)? Does it help you to connect to the others in your scene?
- Does it stimulate your imagination?
- Have you downplayed your objective by using the words "only" or "just?" (I *only* want her to listen. I *just* want to frustrate him.) If so, remove these words.

Additional Thoughts for the Director

Encouraging actors to raise the stakes can help almost every scene. By doing so, you increase the commitment, focus, and energy level of actors, which immediately makes the scene more interesting. This is a handy note to start with when a scene seems flat overall, but you can't put your finger on a specific flaw.

Improvisations are a quick way to jumpstart a scene. Whisper new, heightened circumstances to one or more of the actors. Or secretly give each actor a stronger objective. Let them play the scene exploring and responding to the new conditions. Encourage them to work physically, even starting with just movement and adding the words once the actors have connected to what they are doing. You want them to raise the stakes both intellectually and physically. If actors throw themselves into this exercise, it can generate many useful ideas as well as serving to renew their enthusiasm about working on a scene.

Other Notes of Interest

Take a risk.

Follow your impulse.

You are holding back emotionally.

If the stakes are already there in the text, then that's less work for you. But if not, you have to find something compelling about the character or the story that allows you to raise your own stakes as an actor.

—Karen Ziemba

■ Note

Look for the opposite.

Play the duality.

The Problem

The actor has chosen obvious actions for his character and overlooked opposite impulses.

Explanation

There are many situations in life where we may not know for sure what we want. Perhaps our emotions tell us to do one thing, and our morals or ethics tell us to do another. Or, we know we will be judged harshly by others if we pursue our true desires. Fear, insecurity, and even indecision often interfere in our ability to clearly determine what to do. The result is that two opposite impulses fight against one another. "I want to do it." versus "I don't want to do it." or "I *shouldn't* want to do it." For example, you may want to push a lover away, but on another level you may want to draw her close again. Even if someone has hurt you and you want to get her out of your life, your strong reaction indicates she must matter very deeply to you. Perhaps you are afraid to lose her and have some hope of restoring your relationship. You feel compelled to protect yourself from being hurt again, and yet you want to reach out to her and make yourself vulnerable. Choosing between these two options is difficult, for neither choice is completely satisfactory. Until you are able to make a clear decision, you are torn between conflicting feelings. Moments where we face these dilemmas are multileveled and rich in feeling and thought. It is no surprise that playwrights often have characters struggle with two opposing ideas.

Sometimes it is easy to identify these moments; a character may directly admit he has some hesitations or ambiguous feelings about his situation. He may confess this in a monologue or even openly debate his opposing views with other characters. Often, however, a character may clearly state one desire in his lines while secretly wanting its opposite. For example, a character may outwardly support a friend, while inwardly being envious, hoping his friend will fail. All appearances indicate that he wants to be a loyal friend, for he speaks only words of encouragement. Underneath the surface he may feel guilty for his hidden thoughts, but he has trouble stopping them. In this case, the actor must discover the hidden impulse through textual analysis and experimentation in rehearsal. If the underlying struggle is ignored, only a superficial and simplistic interpretation of the character is possible. The complexity of the moment is lost.

Strategies

The first step is to determine whether your character is wrestling with opposing actions. Look for the climactic moments in the scene and, as your character, identify what you want. Ask yourself if there is any reason to question what you are doing.

- Are there consequences to your action that scare you?
- Do you have a hidden agenda?
- Are you trying to fulfill the expectations of others, even if they are different from your own?
- Do you have doubts or hesitations regarding what you want?
- Does the opposite action interest you?

As you play the scene, create an inner monologue for yourself. Let the voices of the two sides compete for your favor. There will be moments when you hear one voice, e.g., "Forgive him," and moments when you hear the opposite, e.g., "Make him feel guilty." As you struggle, the question of which impulse will win out remains. You may come to a decision within the scene, and you may not. It is the inner conflict that keeps the audience intrigued.

Additional Thoughts for the Director

Many actors neglect to explore opposites on their own, instead favoring actions that are obvious and easy to play. By asking the actor questions about the character's inner fears and desires, you can get him to consider a broader spectrum of possibilities. Encourage the exploration of the opposite impulse by experimenting with the moment. Have the actor go back and forth, first playing the obvious impulse and then playing its opposite. Keep going like a game of Ping-Pong, until you find some middle ground. In this way, the actor will begin to find the rich duality in the situation.

Other Notes of Interest

Find the vulnerability.

Look for the humor.

I have something I call the 180 degree rule. In a healthy process, as soon as we've found something that works I say, 'Good. Let's try it from the exact opposite angle. So if you've just been yelling and angry, let's try caressing and loving, using the same dialogue.' Or, 'If your first impulse is this, that's great, let's act on that impulse. Good. Now let's try its opposite.' The hope is you can find both colors. You start realizing there are many more twists and turns the character is going through emotionally than you thought at first.

—Bill Rauch

■ Note

Look for the humor.

Find the humor in the situation.

It is too serious too soon.

Lighten up.

The Problem

The actor is only playing the serious side of the situation.

Explanation

Human nature is inherently funny. Our lives are filled with irony and hidden comic meaning. The *humor* of life is what keeps us going; it is part of the *human* condition. Good playwrights know this and build it into their scripts. Humor is not limited to comic scripts alone; there is often a great deal of humor even in the most tragic of stories. Most of the first three acts of Shakespeare's *Romeo and Juliet* are filled with good humor. It is only when Mercutio accidentally gets killed that the play starts to turn toward tragedy. Tennessee Williams' poetic drama *A Streetcar Named Desire* has a great deal of humor; most of it comes from Stanley Kowalski's abrasive behavior. Many of Anton Chekhov's plays are considered "comedies," but actors fall prey to the sorrow in Chekhov's characters' situations. They play the entire story with pity and sentiment for their character and wind up with a very flat, dramatic performance. Regardless of whether the play is a comedy or a drama, actors need to find the human element in their characterizations. There will be humorous ideas and situations in almost every play, be it a Greek tragedy or a realistic drama.

Strategies

If you are having trouble finding lighter moments in your role, start by examining your character's relationship to humor. As the character, ask yourself:

- What do you find funny? What makes you laugh?
- Which characters amuse or entertain you?
- How do you make other characters laugh or smile?

Once you have a better picture of your sense of humor, look for comic moments throughout the play. Jokes and comic bits are easy to identify, but a playwright can embed humor in a script in many less obvious ways. Carefully consider all the following:

- use of wit and wordplay
- use of sarcasm and irony
- when you make someone look foolish (metaphor: you throw a pie in his face)
- when you make yourself look foolish (metaphor: you slip on a banana peel)
- when you do something out of character
- moments of contrast or incongruity
- repetition of words or phrases
- repetition of movements or gestures

Humor usually appears somewhere near the beginning of the play, once the audience has learned enough about the characters to find them amusing. It is important to establish a strong characterization early, so the audience has a reference point for the humor or absurdity in the situation. In this way you are helping them to recognize things that will appear incongruous or out of the ordinary later. To establish your character, look to the relationships you have created with the other characters and to the things that surround you. If these are not well defined, the humor cannot be a natural development of the scene. Just be careful not to add things that provoke the audience to laugh but have little to do with the action. Stick to the text and try to establish patterns of behavior that are consistent within the context of the play.

If you are working on an especially serious script, consider your scenes of crisis and climax. Playwrights often employ humor to relieve the tension in a situation, to give the audience a breather from a dramatic situation. They juxtapose the drama with something light and humorous; they add the human element to the proceedings. If you discover most of your objectives are dark and serious, try to lighten up your performance by offsetting the bleak with something promising. Be cautious of interpreting everything you say at a critical moment as serious. Distinguish what is crucial and meaningful from what is there for contrast, release, or irony. Too much of one thing can spoil the balance.

Additional Thoughts for the Director

Many directors find comic moments more difficult to direct than dramatic ones. It is hard to know what will make an audience laugh. Remind the actors that humor must come out of the situation and the characters and not just be inserted "for a laugh." Listen for comic clichés such as using a funny voice, making fun of how another character says a word or phrase by repeating it sarcastically, which may seem funny in rehearsal but do not always translate successfully to an audience. Look for the timing of physical bits and check whether the execution appears *truthful* or *forced*. Humor is a specific art form, and it needs careful attention to detail to work for the theatre.

Other Notes of Interest

Set up the laugh.

Don't anticipate the laugh.

Look for the opposite.

Humor is such a valuable commodity in the theatre, even in the darkest tragedies. It makes the audience vulnerable. It brings the audience closer to the characters and enables them to become participants. Then the audience can fully take the journey with the actor. Build up the same constant tension and the audience will get tired of it. They'll get physically tired. On the other hand, all rules in the theatre are meant to be broken, aren't they? Just break them brilliantly.

—D. Scott Glasser

Humor makes life able to bear, able to stomach. We have so many terrible things in our lives and in our world. You have to find the other side. How do we live through it, how do we survive? It's because we do laugh, we do find humor in it.

—Karen Ziemba

■ Note

Find the antithesis.

Make the comparison.

The Problem

The actor is missing the antithesis inherent in the text.

Explanation

As far back as the Greeks, the use of antithesis has been an effective tool in playwriting, as a means to debate the issues and themes in a play. All good writers, whether they are poets, novelists, essayists, or columnists, use comparison and contrast in their work. For the stage, antithesis is commonly employed in two ways: to set up the differing viewpoints between characters, or for one character to weigh opposing ideas against one another. Shakespeare continually employed antithesis, not only in dialogue between two characters, but also in his famous characters' soliloquies.

In the most basic of terms, antithesis is employing the direct opposite of a word, phrase, or clause to make a comparison. The comparison is used to offer new meaning or challenge an idea previously thought to be the supposed truth. By juxtaposing two seemingly opposite ideas, the playwright is allowing the characters the opportunity to think in a new way. In a longer speech, antithesis gives the character a means of sorting out a particularly difficult problem by debating the issue with himself. Take Hamlet's famous "To be or not to be" as example. The entire speech is rich in word and phrase comparison. The first line itself "To be or not to be, that is the question" is the set-up for a long string of antithetical ideas, as Hamlet tries to solve his problem out loud, weighing life (action) against death (inaction).

Sometimes it is difficult for an actor to grasp the antithesis in a line or speech, even though we often use comparisons in our everyday conversations. However, a play text is much more structured and, as such, demands a more keen awareness on the part of the actor as to how the language is being used.

Strategies

First, identify the comparisons in the script. Underline in different colors the words or phrases that relate to each other. Now ask yourself the nature of the comparison. How is your character using antithesis? Are you being sarcastic, ironic, witty, funny, or serious? What kind of words do you use to make the comparison? Are they poetic, symbolic, or metaphorical? Finally, ask yourself your reason or objective in using antithesis. What are you trying to accomplish by making the comparison? Are you trying to sway someone's point of view? Bring clarity to your own thoughts on the issue at hand? Persuade an opponent over to your side?

Physicalizing and vocalizing the words can help you see and hear the antithesis in the line. As a rehearsal exercise, set up the words like a weighing scale. Put one idea on the right side of you by using a gesture ("to be"). Then gesture on your left with the other idea ("or not to be"). Follow through by bringing both the right and the left together in a single gesture at the center ("that is the question"). As you do this, use your voice to separate and then bring back together the idea you are trying to express. Use a different tone for each part, right (higher tone), left (lower tone), and then center (middle tone).

Additional Thoughts for the Director

Most inexperienced actors will need some coaching on the use of antithesis. Ask the actor to separate out the most important antithetical statements in the scene. Then have him articulate in his own words his understanding of both sides of the comparison. As you talk, have the actor defend one idea over the other. You may also have him try to personalize the issue by finding a comparison in his own life that is similar to the one being made in the play. When the actor is ready, have him then play the scene using the words of the text. Working this way will ensure a stronger subtext underneath the line and a clearer understanding of the antithetical idea.

Other Notes of Interest

Trust the text.

Make the realization.

Make the transition.

Separate your thoughts.

■ Note

Use more variety in your choices.

You are too predictable.

There is too much sameness.

The Problem

The actor has a tendency to respond to each event in a similar manner.

Explanation

When you have known someone for a very long time, you can almost predict her responses to certain things. "Oh, she wouldn't like that!" or "That would make her very angry!" You think you *really* know someone, and then one day she does something you never thought possible: she chooses to respond in a way you did not anticipate. Part of what makes people fascinating is that they can surprise you.

An actor who plays a character all on one note, with the same emotions, the same pace, and the same responses, will have difficulty creating an exciting performance. Audiences enjoy variety and those moments when a character does something unpredictable.

It is easy to get locked into a limited range of responses. An actor selects a few reactions that are logical to the character, such as "angry," "doubtful," or "forgiving," and fails to explore beyond these choices. All her reactions, vocal choices, and gestures relate to these emotions or states of being. They become an inherent part of her interpretation and she proceeds to use them to get through the entire action of the play, without variety or change. Hence, everything the actor says or does begins to take on a "sameness" or predictability. Rather than engaging in the action of the character, she relies on emotions to guide her in her reactions.

Strategies

If you are attentive to the growth of your character throughout a scene or play, you will automatically begin to vary your responses. Chart your evolution from beginning to end and note when you gain new knowledge, change your perspective, or confront new events. Look for developments in the character's life and for peaks and curves in the action. What happens to you emotionally, physically, and vocally throughout the play? You will see more clearly the range of responses your character has, once you understand the journey your character takes. To keep the journey from being too predictable, it is also important to keep an eye out for the unexpected moments in your character's life. Ask yourself:

- When are you caught off guard?
- When do you have to adjust to new information?
- When must you work on a problem you did not anticipate?
- When are you surprised by something another character says or does?

- When are you harboring a secret?
- When do you act irrationally or surprise yourself?

Examine how your character reacts throughout the play. If Hamlet reacts to everything in the same way, say "bitterly," "angrily," or "madly," then the audience may lose interest in his plight. Once you have selected specific actions, you can apply adverbs to add diversity to your choices. If your response is "to refuse" then try qualifying the intention with something that will either intensify the response such as "to stubbornly refuse" or soften it with "to quietly refuse." Make sure that during the course of one scene you never choose the same adverb twice. This should add variety to your overall objective and open yourself up to less obvious choices.

Additional Thoughts for the Director

Every actor has a bag of tricks, those emotions and qualities that truly work for her on stage. While this is an indication of someone who is comfortable with herself when performing, it can also mean that she is afraid to abandon the tried and true for something new. Variety adds spice to life. Ask the actor to try and bring something new into rehearsal, by having her reexamine her overall objective. Even a slight word adjustment in that objective may bring new and dynamic choices to the forefront.

Other Notes of Interest

Don't play the ending.

Concentrate on the action, not the emotion.

Look for the opposite.

Look for the humor.

Use more variety in your choices, to me wouldn't mean anything. I would need something more specific. Now if a director gave me a very technical note such as, 'Use more variety in your pitch,' that's a very objective note, entirely technical. Then it would be my homework to figure out why the pitches would have to be more varied.

—Linda Purl

■ Note

Use the images.

Let the words affect you.

Believe in the imagery.

The Problem

The actor is overlooking the pictures, feelings, and images contained in the language.

Explanation

An artist paints with colors; a playwright paints with words. A good playwright takes great care to select expressive words and phrases that are appropriate to the character and situation. Part of the actor's job is to thoroughly examine the text and to become aware of a character's use of language. An actor who ignores the specificity of the language or merely takes the words for granted will miss a great deal of the richness of his role. Word choice can reveal what is going on inside a character—how the character is struggling to express ideas, his emotional state, or his perception of the world around him. The word images illustrate and make vivid the mental images of the character. Strong images can assault the senses. By investigating the language and the imagery it contains, one can find clear clues about how to play a character and about what makes him unique. The next step is to translate this language from symbols on a page into spoken expression.

It is easy to muddle through a part, getting the plot out without giving the language much weight. However, for the play to be effective, the words need to come alive and be channeled through the character. If an actor does not pay attention to the specificity of his words, or if he does not bring the images in the text to life, the audience will not be moved. However, if the actor allows the emotional and sensual content of the words to affect him and color his delivery, both the character and the play as a whole will be more powerful.

If an actor's line delivery seems flat or uninspired, he has probably not investigated the language in any depth. Instead, the actor frequently paraphrases his lines or replaces significant words with synonyms. If the language has no significance to the actor, if he is merely keeping the story going, the delivery of the lines will more than likely be lifeless.

Strategies

The first obvious step in tapping into the power of the words and imagery is to analyze the text.

- Which words and phrases evoke emotional, visual, or physical reactions?
- Which words are particularly descriptive?

- Which words are unique to the character?
- How does the character's language change at climactic moments?

Pay attention to the words as you say them and notice how one image or idea leads to the next. Allow yourself time to experiment with the language, playing with varying your inflection, speed, volume, and expression. Enjoy saying the words and let them guide you in your explorations. Become familiar with the language and comfortable with saying it.

There are several approaches to dealing with word imagery. The first is to study it from a visual standpoint. Identify what pictures the words conjure up. If the character is describing an event, place, or feeling, have a *specific* visual image in your mind. Close your eyes and see the scenery, the colors, and the shapes. Make it as vivid and as real to you as possible. As you say the words, try to paint a picture for those who are listening—get them to see what you are seeing. Let the words be springboards to creating the visual image.

You may also work with words aurally, dealing with the sounds they contain. Listen for the difference between harsher plosive consonants such as 'p's and 'b's and softer fricatives such as 'f's and 'v's. What feeling or texture do they inspire? Find sounds which go at a clip, which attack and bite, or which linger at a slow pace. Each consonant has a unique quality, and each combination of consonants creates a unique impression. Likewise, paying attention to vowel sounds will give you a lot of information. Long, open sounds have a vastly different emotional impact from short vowel sounds. Explore the differences. Finally, look for onomatopoeia, where the words sound like what they mean. Let the sounds of the words affect you and help you to detect the underlying meaning of what you are saying.

The third approach is physical and kinetic. Experiment with the imagery in the language through movement. Physicalize what you are saying and then verbalize it. This may mean miming an image or actually acting it out. It may mean reacting to the words in an abstract way, letting the body capture the essence of the image in a physical gesture. You may choose to speak as you explore physically, or you can let the body find the physical expression first and then add the words. When you go back to the words with the actual blocking, you will find that the language is more vivid to you and you are connecting to what you are saying in a physical way.

Last, it is crucial for you to have a deep understanding of the meaning of your words. Be sure to look up any unfamiliar words, but also take time to investigate words you think you know well. Take some of the character's most important words, go to the dictionary, and read all the definitions. Does a definition make a word clearer to you? Are there secondary meanings, which give you new insight into what the character is saying? Once you have a full grasp of meanings, you are less likely to rush through your lines blindly. This will help you to see why a character chooses certain words for the images they evoke.

Additional Thoughts for the Director

Your enthusiasm for the language of the play can help to inspire the actors and instill in them an appreciation of the playwright's craft. When you discuss a scene, point out its language and images. Ask the actors how that language impresses them, how the images relate to the theme of the play, and what overall mood is evoked. As you rehearse, if an actor overlooks an important word or phrase, coach him to put quotation marks around the idea. This technique helps the actor to highlight words and forces him to give what he is saying more weight.

Other Notes of Interest

Find the antithesis.

Emphasize key words.

■ Note

Differentiate your characters when playing multiple roles.

The Problem

Each character the actor is portraying lacks an individual presence and needs more dimension and complexity.

Explanation

Some producing directors use multiple-role casting to keep costs down. It is more economical to hire one actor who can play many roles than to cast each role individually. This is especially true in productions of Shakespeare's plays, which often require doubling, as well as most productions of Dickens' *A Christmas Carol.*

Some texts are written specifically for one actor to play many roles. This is a theatrical device that can be a very effective technique for giving depth and dimension to a situation or story. The device can also be entertaining and engaging to an audience. Some examples are the dentist (who also is written to play numerous other characters) in the musical *The Little Shop of Horrors* or the two actors who play multiple characters in the comedy *Greater Tuna*.

Many actors are very adept at taking on a number of different parts at the same time. Actors hired for a season of plays at a regional or repertory theatre, such as The Guthrie in Minneapolis or Steppenwolf in Chicago, are expected to have this skill. The task of differentiating characters is generally easier in this situation, as the actor is playing a number of different parts in a season of plays; each has a unique set of given circumstances requiring a specific style of acting. But when the actor is faced with performing a number of roles in the same play, the task of differentiating becomes more difficult.

In facing the challenge of playing multiple characters, many actors make general rather than specific choices. They grab on to just one simple choice, when what is needed is a multifaceted approach. But an audience is not easily deceived, and this technique may actually call attention to the fact that the actor is playing a number of different parts. A common trap for an actor is to use one basic character and overlay a single distinguishing characteristic on top, for instance, by making an obvious physical or vocal adjustment for each character. Other actors choose to use emotion as a means of differentiation, by playing different aspects of the same personality type for each role. The only adjustment they make for each character is in emotional quality or delivery. Though they are playing different emotions, the character remains the same.

Sometimes actors can wind up playing characters that are similar to their own personality. They use themselves as the base and apply one adjective to the character type to help them differentiate each scene (i.e., the "uptight" character, the "frantic" character, the "angry" character). In the end, this will also call attention to the fact that the same actor is playing a number of different parts.

Strategies

Playing multiple roles can be both challenging and exciting for you. Approach each character with imagination and creativity. Every effort should be made to make each character you play a unique individual. Physical and vocal adjustments are important, but rather than choosing the obvious, such as a physical "limp" or vocal "nasality," try to make your choices more complex and specific. The first place to look is in the text itself. Are there hidden clues which will help you to distinguish each character? Go back to some basic questions you should ask of every character you undertake:

- What do you say about yourself?
- What do others say about you?
- What do your actions reveal?
- What is your perspective on life?
- What is your status in the situation?
- How do you relate to others around you? Are you an introvert or an extrovert? More confident or insecure? More aggressive or restrained?

Try to translate this information into a physical choice, which you can use as a hook before you go on stage. Does your character lead from a specific part of the body? How does your choice affect your posture? Your breathing? Your focus?

You may decide to rehearse with an individual costume piece or personal prop, such as a hat, a pair of glasses, gloves, or a cloak. This will help you to distinguish one character from another and give you something tangible to work with. However, it is important to remember that your accessory should not become a crutch. Once you have decided on the specific costume or prop, make sure you discover how the character uses it and why it is important to her. Remember the more you differentiate your characters with informed and complex choices, the more successful the performance will be in the end.

Additional Thoughts for the Director

Organization is key. Have the actor playing multiple roles make a chart of each of her character's entrances and exits. On the chart, have her specify where each of the characters is coming from and where each intends on going. She can then use this chart as a springboard for specificity. Have her include such information as what has just happened to her, what her attitude is toward others, and what energy she brings with her. Help the actor to clarify her purpose in the scene and her relative importance to the action of the play.

Other Notes of Interest

Do your homework.

Give focus/take focus.

Take control.

Take the stage.

It is about telling stories; it's not about displaying acting. It does not necessarily mean every time you walk out on to the stage, your mother can't recognize you. So you don't have to create a mask every time you go out. Yet, the basic psychological center of the characters wants to be markedly different. That does not necessarily mean that the voice has to be a character voice from person to person, or that a lot of the mechanics of acting need to be on display. You shouldn't be different just to be different. It isn't bad to get into say false dentures, wigs etc., but the motivation has to be pure.

—Joseph Hanreddy

The Notes

Pace and Flow

■ Note

Act on the lines, not in between them.

Take out the pause.

The Problem

The actor is using pauses between lines to think through, react to, and discover ideas.

Explanation

Pauses can be very seductive. Actors often enjoy using silence to heighten moments since reactions seem to have more resonance when isolated in time. Occasional, well-placed pauses can grab the audience's attention and be extremely effective. However, too many pauses can be deadly and destroy the momentum of the story and the pace of the performance.

An actor may get caught in the habit of pausing each time he has a reaction. In other words, an actor says a line and then takes time for his character to respond. His realizations, emotions, actions, even physicalizations take place in between lines. "To be or not to be" becomes "To be" (pause to ponder, turn head, get idea) "or not to be" (realize the dilemma, draw a conclusion, walk across the stage). Rather than moving a scene forward with rhythm and flow, this actor slows it down

104

to: speak, act, speak, act. Although it may feel to him that he is working carefully through each moment, he is actually chopping up any sense of continuity. The acting may also appear indulgent, that he is showing off his deep thought. Those same reactions and physicalizations, when *tied to the words,* become much more powerful and restore the flow of the scene.

In early stages of rehearsal, it is useful to slow down the pace of dialogue as actors investigate and draw conclusions about the scene. The actor may take time to reflect on what is happening around him or figure out tactics or an inner monologue. Pauses may occur as an actor "catches up" with the thought process of his character. Once an actor has become acquainted with a scene, the pauses disappear and he is able to think as quickly as his character. However, if the actor gets accustomed to having extra time for contemplation and holds onto the pauses, the scene will struggle to achieve a realistic pace.

Strategies

If you find it necessary to react *after* you have said a line, go back to the line and analyze it.

- Which words or phrases trigger your reaction?
- Which words bring you to a discovery, a conclusion, or a realization?

Allow your reactions to be played *as you say the words* that triggered them. Your character's thoughts and feelings need to occur simultaneously with the words you speak. You can still take time, but *while* you speak the text rather than after the fact. Savor words, play with them, and let ideas hit you as you say them. Connect your breath with your impulse to speak. Breathe in new thoughts and let the words immediately follow, rather than taking a breath to think about an idea and then inhaling again to speak. If you discover your lover has betrayed you, let the outrage, disgust, and humiliation all surface as you say the word "betrayed." You can stretch the word out and let it resonate.

Indulging in pauses may mean you have placed too much attention on yourself—your own reactions and performance—rather than on your relationship to the other characters in the scene. Fight to express yourself and affect your partners; this is hard to do if you are constantly interrupting the flow of your thoughts. Adjusting your focus from yourself to your scene partners can quickly eliminate unnecessary pauses.

Additional Thoughts for the Director

Remember, in the initial stages of the rehearsal process, actors are more inclined to use pauses as they consider choices and get a handle on their roles. Allow them time to learn and experiment before addressing this note. If an actor has an unnecessary pause, question him about his inner monologue. What is he thinking at that moment? Is he regrouping? Changing tactics? Responding to new information? Once the actor is able to articulate his reason for the pause, coach him to channel the intent into the words. The meaning of the pause then becomes the subtext of his lines.

Other Notes of Interest

> Earn the pause.
> Pick up the pace.

■ Note

> Earn the pause.
> Build to a pause.

The Problem

The actor uses pauses indiscriminately, either too often, or without need, undermining their effectiveness.

Explanation

Pauses are a natural part of our speech patterns, necessary as we search for ideas, either as we process what is said to us or as we regroup after difficult moments. When used on the stage, pauses can be dramatically powerful, heightening the tension in a scene and keeping the audience on the edge of their seats. They also can provide time for the audience to catch their breath and make sense of what is going on.

Pauses are not dead air. They come out of what is happening between the characters and are as integral to the scene as to the dialogue. Effective pauses are triggered by necessity; they appear when no words are possible. Whether they are relatively short pauses or longer, more substantial pauses, if they are not the result of a strong need they will have no energy or impact and will detract from the scene.

A pause can be necessitated by many factors. A character may have just faced a crisis and needs time to compose herself and think. The rhythm of the scene may have built to a climax, the emotional weight of the moment may need a release, or the physicality of the scene may have reached a point of exhaustion. A pause grows out of the action and effort preceding it. It exists on its own, often functioning as an unspoken line of dialogue, a line which is unnecessary to hear but important to feel and watch.

A common mistake of actors is to use pauses too frequently. Because pauses create dynamic and exciting moments, it is tempting to place them throughout a scene. But the result is that too many pauses quickly cancel each other out. The first pause or two may work, but subsequent pauses lose their value because they are no longer unique. The pace of the scene drags; the action is broken up by blank spaces that have no significance.

Strategies

Understanding the rhythm of the scene will help you to sense where pauses will be effective. Pauses result from action, so they usually reside at the end of a beat. Placing several pauses earlier on in a beat will undermine the potency of a pause at the end. This does not mean that a pause cannot come midway through a beat, but it still must be triggered by something specific. Figure where you really need it, where a pause will be most powerful, and cut pauses in other places.

To ensure that a pause is meaningful, you can label it with a catchword or phrase describing what is happening at that moment. This can help you to identify why the pause exists and what purpose it serves. If you cannot find a label or determine its function, eliminate the pause. Some examples of labels are:

- regroup
- compose self
- time to think
- take it all in
- stand my ground
- search for what to say
- summon my courage
- situation at impasse

Additional Thoughts for the Director

Rather than giving this as a general note to an actor, be very clear as to where you think there are too many pauses, and then rehearse those specific moments. First, point out the pauses you mutually agree upon and then tighten up the cues where a pause does not seem appropriate to the action of the scene. When the actor takes an unnecessary pause, have her immediately go back and repeat the moment, putting the action on the line rather than before or after it. Try to get a rhythm going, don't let the actor stop and discuss the moment, just keep the scene moving. You may also want the actors to try a speed-through of the lines to experience the script without any pauses.

Other Notes of Interest

Act on the lines, not in between them.

> Sometimes a pause, a moment of stillness can knock your socks off. You stop for a second because you don't know what to say, or you're thinking of the next part of the story you want to tell. Your mind is going a million miles an hour, yet you can't talk.
>
> —Karen Ziemba

> Maybe it is about earning the pause, but it's also about rhythm. Pauses have no meaning or value if there are too many of them.
>
> —Bill Rauch

■ Note

> Pick up the pace.
> Pick up your cues.
> Think faster.

The Problem

A scene moves too slowly and loses the audience's interest.

Explanation

Pace can be a problem any time during the rehearsal period, but it often arises as a show approaches opening night. Many a director, after a long run-through, has been known to say: "the show is dragging," "we are running ten minutes too long," or "everything has to move much faster!" Any play, no matter how brilliant or well acted, can suffer if it moves too slowly.

Pace doesn't necessarily correspond to speed. A scene can seem slow for a variety of reasons. Yes, it can be that lines are spoken too slowly. But more often than not, the actual speed of the show is fine, but other elements interfere to drag down the *perceived* pace. Here are a few possible reasons:

- Actors are tired or have low energy.
- Actors aren't picking up cues, leaving "dead" gaps between lines.
- Actors aren't excited by their choices; the stakes aren't high enough.
- The cast isn't working as a team; actors are concentrating on their own moments and not paying enough attention to or reacting off of other actors.
- There isn't enough variety in a scene.

Strategies

If you are given a note to pick up the pace, try to think faster rather than just moving or speaking faster. Be on your toes and stay intently focused. Think of picking up your cues, as similar to a game of volleyball. The only way to win is to work as a team. Use your lines as you would use the volleyball. One actor gets in a response to a good serve, another one keeps the ball up in the air and sets up the next actor who smashes it over the net. Remember that a good team player is always paying attention, waiting alertly for the return, always keeping an eye on the ball. This kind of metaphor will help to energize the scene and keep the action moving forward.

To help you to come in more quickly with your cues, look for what triggers each line. Is there a particular word or phrase, a gesture or expression from another character that gives you the urge to speak? Find that impulse, connect it to your breath and then let that drive your response. A good playwright provides you a motivation to speak, and if you springboard off of it, your lines will have the right timing and pace.

Additional Thoughts for the Director

If pace seems to be a problem, a physical activity, such as tossing a ball, may help to energize the cast. Have the actors toss the ball back and forth during a particularly difficult sequence in the dialogue. The actor with the first line starts the game. As he speaks his text, he keeps the ball moving, tossing it from one hand to the other. When he gets to the end of his text, he tosses the ball to the actor who has the next line, and so forth. If someone drops the ball, either the group starts the sequence over or the actor repeats his line until he makes a successful toss. Remind the actors to connect this physical activity to their breath as well as to their words.

Other Notes of Interest

> Raise the stakes.
>
> Use more variety in your choices.
>
> Earn the pause.
>
> Don't rush.
>
> Connect with your scene partner.

If pace is a problem, generally speaking, the director should put it in words 'there's not enough at stake' or 'the objective is not strong enough,' 'the action is not one that has any personal meaning to the actors or characters.' As an actor, you are forever trying to find things that will, in fact, propel you forward. Nine times out of ten, actual speed means nothing, because you can go really fast and be just as bad as you can be. We have all seen those actors who are rushing, but that's all they are doing, rushing, and it doesn't really mean anything.

—Boyd Gaines

■ Note

> Don't rush.
>
> Slow down.
>
> Pace yourself.

The Problem

The actor is rushing through the words and actions, thus losing subtlety and details inherent in the text.

Explanation

Being in a rush is a way of life for many people. We measure success by our accomplishments: how many things we have done, places we have gone to, or people we have seen in a day. Sometimes the quantity of our work is seen as more important than its quality. But in our active daily lives, there is not always an audience trying to watch, follow, and share in our actions. It can be a challenge for an actor who is used to speeding through her own life, to slow down once she is on the stage.

There are a number of reasons why actors tend to rush through a moment or scene; the most common is nervous energy. When stage fright takes over and stress levels are high, a performance can easily slip out of the control of the actor. It is not uncommon for an actor, fraught with nerves, to think, "I just want to get through this and get it over with!" All the detailed work done in rehearsal, all the subtleties and refinements, are forgotten as the actor tries to get to the end of a speech as fast and painlessly as possible. Another reason an actor might rush over a section is she is unclear about its meaning. She may hurry past a moment hoping that the audience will not notice her uncertainty or discomfort. This particularly happens with verse or classical texts.

When an actor is rushing, most often it has nothing to do with the actual pace of her performance. An experienced actor can move through a speech leisurely or at lightning speed, whichever rate is appropriate, without sacrificing clarity or nuance. It is when an actor hurries through her ideas, not completing one thought before moving on to the next, that it seems she is rushing. Let's say an actor has a sequence of thoughts, justifying betraying her family. Her first statement is, "I was mistreated by my parents," but she says this so quickly, without ever taking the idea in, digesting it, or allowing it to resonate, that it comes across as unimportant to her. It makes no impact on the audience because they have no time to process what she has said. She does the same thing with the next idea, "I was never appreciated." Again, this is passed over so easily that it does not seem to mean anything to her. She gets through the speech successfully, but because she does not take time to finish any of her thoughts, truly think about what she is saying, or let it affect her, she ends up glossing over the richness and depth of her past history and consequently loses the ability to move the audience.

Strategies

Relaxation is key in helping you gain control over your performance. Simple stretches, physical activity, breathing exercises, or meditations prior to a show can calm your mind and prevent you from rushing. The less tension and stress you feel, the better prepared you will be to keep your nerves at bay. If you catch yourself rushing in the middle of a performance, taking a deep breath can be an effective way to slow down your pulse and clear your head. Ground yourself by feeling your feet on the floor, making eye contact with your scene partner and listening more carefully to what is going on.

If there is a specific section of a scene you tend to speed through, check your understanding of the text. Do you know exactly what you are saying and why you are saying it? Have you worked through each individual thought? Move through your speech slowly, one step at a time, fully exploring each idea and its implications. Most often you will find you have only played the surface of an idea, overlooking some elements of your thought process. You can also experiment by running the scene as fast as you possibly can, immediately following this by running the scene at normal speed. You may find the contrast between the two will help you to settle into a less frenzied pace.

Additional Thoughts for the Director

Merely making the actor aware she is rushing may not be enough to solve the problem. Rather, check to make sure she understands what she means with her words and, more important, why she chooses this particular moment to say them. Help her articulate the subtext, the underlying meaning of her lines. Clarify the beat shifts of the scene with the actor, and discuss how each beat has a unique energy and pace.

You might try asking the actors to vary their rhythms. Clap out a variety of rhythms as the actors run the scene. As you clap, experiment with slowing moments down and speeding others up. Help the actors to distinguish which moments work best at a fast pace and which benefit from taking more time.

Other Notes of Interest

Don't anticipate the moment.

Don't play the ending.

Separate your thoughts.

■ Note

Enter/exit dynamically.

Where are you coming from? Going to?

Take your energy into the wings.

The Problem

The actor's entrance or exit needs to carry more dramatic weight.

Explanation

In their rush to focus on the meat of a scene, actors often overlook the opportunities that exist when a character walks on or off the stage. Every entrance is a new moment, a beginning in and of itself, just as an exit serves as a punctuation or finish. A carefully played entrance or exit can further the plot, enhance the text, and especially add detail and distinction to a characterization. However, when actors neglect to pay attention to these moments, the result can range from a small drop in the scene's energy to a character losing believability for the audience.

Ignoring the importance of an entrance or exit is a common mistake. The actor always needs to take into consideration the life of the character offstage, where he is coming from or going to, and allow this information to affect his behavior. Some actors come onto stage "cold" and start responding as their characters only after they have been in the scene for a few seconds. This means for the first few moments of their appearance they were not truly in character, a fault that the audience quickly senses. Likewise, if an actor drops out of character as he walks off the stage—perhaps he starts to think about his next costume change or secretly reviews how the scene went while he is still visible to the audience—it can undermine the effectiveness of his performance.

Conversely, an actor can take into account his character's life offstage and still have an entrance or exit that comes across as "flat." For instance, an entrance may not equal or add to the energy already established in the scene and thus slow down its momentum. The pace or commitment level may be too low. Or the entrance may need something extra, something specific to establish the character's presence and purpose. An exit, for example, may lack a sense of completion or finality. The actor may end his performance with his last line and fail to use the exit as a transition into the next moment of the play.

Strategies

Having it pointed out to you, that an entrance or exit is "missing something," sometimes can be enough to focus your attention and trigger an instinctive solution. By intensifying your energy and commitment to your character at that specific moment, you will find ideas will occur to you as you play the situation.

Knowing where your character is coming from or going to is crucial. Be specific about what your character is thinking, doing, and feeling before you enter, and assume those traits prior to stepping onto the stage. What has happened to your character since your last appearance, and how do these events affect you? Think about your scene beginning not at your entrance, but offstage, so that by the time you can be seen by the audience you are fully connected to your character and in the *middle* of playing your action. Likewise, it is important to determine what your character is planning to do as you leave. Consider what the other characters have done or said to you that cause you to exit. Carry this intention off with you and stay in character a few steps beyond where you can no longer be seen. Most of us have had the experience of watching a character exit the scene only to see the actor drop out of character while still in view. This spoils the illusion.

If you have to wait a long time to make an entrance, you may face the problem of being physically energized. Each actor discovers a way that works best for him, but some common choices are shaking/swinging arms and limbs, jumping or running in place, or stretching. Some actors like to interact with other actors backstage, whether this be to gear up physically, to run dialogue, or to improvise in character.

If you want to make your entrance or exit more distinctive, consider how it can help to reveal aspects of your character. The best choices will come out of the particular circumstances of your character and the play, but here are some generic ideas to stimulate your thinking:

- What information are you bringing onto the stage or carrying off of the stage?
- Are you trying to communicate something to the other characters as you move?
- What do you want the other characters to believe about you? Are you hiding something?
- Is your pace slow, medium, or fast? Does the pace change midway through your entrance/exit?
- How does your character's posture change at that moment?
- Is there a prop your character would relate to? Any physical business that would be appropriate?
- Is the walk smooth, choppy, composed, carefree, or restricted?
- Where or at whom do you look?

Additional Thoughts for the Director

The simplest solution to this problem is to tell the actor to think about the entrance or exit in question. Have the actor run the entrance and/or exit a number of times and vary the intention until one "hits" and seems to elevate the moment. You can also have the actors run *just* the entrances and exits of each scene or act. This will help them to fully appreciate the comings and goings of all the characters in the play. Ask

the actors to improvise in rehearsal the "moment before" of an entrance
or the "moment after" of an exit to give them specific details to focus
on when in performance.

Other Notes of Interest

Energize the beginning of the scene.

> Do not come onto the stage without an idea. If you're not aspiring
> to something or to someone—don't come on the stage. Wait, if you
> must. But don't come to the stage and then be without an objective.
> —André De Shields

> You have to be careful because sometimes you can get into a bad habit
> of taking entrances and exits for the sake of doing something dramatic.
> It's just about where are you coming from, what you're coming into,
> where are you going. That's going to tell you how you enter or how
> you exit.
> —Scott Ellis

■ Note

> Set up the laugh.
> Work on your timing of the joke.

The Problem

The actor is having difficulty executing a joke or comic bit of business.

Explanation

Comedy is a universal language. Everybody loves a good joke. Wherever
we are, whomever we meet, we tend to remember the funny things
that happen to us and the amusing things people say and do. Everyone
likes to get the laugh, to say the line that brings down the house. In the
theatre, some roles require actors to set up the jokes, while others get to
deliver the punch lines. Many successful comedy teams have built their
reputation on the straight-man/funny-man motif: Abbott and Costello,
Laurel and Hardy, Martin and Lewis, Penn and Teller, Hope and Crosby.
There are also famous male–female teams such as Lucille Ball and Desi
Arnaz, George Burns and Gracie Allen, Imogene Coco and Sid Caesar.
The comedy is in the reactions, from both the straight man and the

funny man. To this day, good situation comedy is based on this kind of familiar character interaction.

Strategies

Comedy is all about precision and timing. Great comics will say they were not funny because their "timing was off." There are many ways to work on the timing of a joke. First, identify who you think is going to get the laugh; in other words, who is the "straight man" and who is the "funny man." The focus on stage should always be on the person who has the punch line.

Next, you need to identify what kind of humor you are playing. Physical comedy is exactly that, physical. In fact, a lot of humor occurs in silence. Most of the second act of the comedy *Noises Off* is a series of physical mishaps as the "actors" try to keep the action of the play going "onstage," while trying to be quiet "backstage." For slapstick humor, the laugh will be from the physical timing of the body in motion. To work on your physical timing, ask yourself a few key questions:

- Are you anticipating a move such as a trip, slap, fall, hit, or "spit take" (the character spits out liquid just after taking a sip because the other character said or did something ridiculous)?
- Does the moment require a take (a quick look to the other actor and then out to the audience) or double take (two quick looks in succession)?
- Is the pause between physical bits too long or too short?
- What are the rhythm and pace of the sequence of events?

Wit, wordplay, and puns require a different kind of timing. A joke is all about the juxtaposition of words. Consider these questions:

- Are your lines exact? Do you have the playwright's sequence correct?
- Are you swallowing the words or articulating them with precision?
- Are you coming in too early or too late with the next line? Does the moment require either a short pause or a long pause between lines?
- Are you punching the right word at the right time to make the joke comprehensible?
- Does the last word of the joke need an upward inflection (question) or an even or downward inflection (answer)?

Also look for word repetition in the lines. The very familiar "who's on first" routine developed by Abbott and Costello is all about the misinterpretation of a series of repeated phrases: "who" being on first base, "what" being on second base, and "I don't know" being on third base. The repetition of these phrases, delivered with more frustration and conviction, gives the piece its humor. This classic routine is also built on the comedic rule of "three." Sequences of three are often used successfully to achieve humor. Search for combinations of three words, phrases or movements, and identify how they work together. Does the first lead to the second, the second set up the third, and the third serve as the punch line?

The audience can give you quick feedback. If they miss a word, if they can't see what's happening, if the pauses are too long, they won't respond. Let the audience teach you about timing. Whether you are in a farce, full of door slams, dropping pants, and slapstick humor, or in a Restoration comedy rich with razor wit and ingenious word play, the timing of the humor is essential to getting the laugh.

Additional Thoughts for the Director

Working on comedy is a serious business. Plays with a great deal of comedy require great attention to detail. Allow the time in rehearsal to work out the timing of a specific bit of business or routine. Give the actors free reign to explore the timing on their own. Remind the actors that the characters don't know they are being funny. Comedy is about teamwork. Be a guide and not a dictator, but remind the actors that you have the same perspective as the audience. When it comes to timing, they need to rely on your judgment.

Other Notes of Interest

Build vocally.

Don't anticipate the laugh.

Look for the humor.

Play through to the crest of the laughter or applause.

Set up somebody else's laugh, that's key for an actor. It's difficult to play the straight man, sometimes, but that's what your job is; that's what Dean Martin's job was with Jerry Lewis. It can be very satisfying when somebody else gets a laugh because of something that you've done. That's a collaboration as well, an actor collaboration. When a director sets a great tone, it allows the actors to have trust not only in the director, but in the other actors as well, and they will want to make things work as a *whole piece*.

—Karen Ziemba

There is not going to be a lot of discussion in a note session for a comedy. There will be pages of notes, but they go fast, because they are all about timing and props.

—Joseph Hanreddy

The basic rule of thumb with comedy is know who has got the laugh, and look at that person.

—Boyd Gaines

■ Note

Play through to the crest of the laughter or applause.

You are stepping on the laugh.

You are killing the applause.

The Problem

The actors are either not holding through the crest of the audience response or waiting too long for that response to die down before continuing the action.

Explanation

Audience response will vary from performance to performance, whether it is a comedy, a drama, or a musical. In front of an audience, actors have the opportunity to find out how the timing of laughs and applause is truly working. Directors often remind the cast beforehand to play through to the crest of the laughter or applause to keep the show moving; otherwise, they may "step" on a laugh or "kill" the applause. Often the actors are not clear as to what this means or how to do it.

The crest of an audience response is akin to a wave breaking onto the shore. At a certain moment, the wave reaches its high peak and then curls over and breaks. This force propels the water toward the shore where it dissipates and is then drawn back out into the ocean. The moment just after the break is called the "crest" of the wave, and it is typically the moment when the actor resumes the playing of action after a laugh or applause. Like the wave, an audience response is a phenomenon that can be measured in size and sound.

In live theatre, audience response is an important part of the theatrical event. Laughter is the most commonly "heard" response from an audience, and it is an especially good indicator that they are paying attention, enjoying the play, and grasping the humor or irony in the situation. For laughter, timing is crucial. Think for a moment about a good comic; he learns to "play the audience" by coming in with the punch line just at the moment when the audience is ripe and ready to hear it. He holds the moment just until the laughter has peaked before moving on to the next joke. A good comic never lets the laughter die down completely, or the pace of the show suffers. If the laughter is cut off, the audience will subconsciously stop laughing, for fear they will miss out on something. Waiting too long or cutting off the applause too soon means the audience will be less inclined to applaud for any substantial amount of time as the show continues.

Strategies

Listening is your best strategy; you need almost a split focus when performing. Remember you are listening both as a character and as a performer. As a character, you listen and respond "in the moment" to the action of the play. As a performer, you need to listen and respond to the effect your performance has on the audience. Some laughs will be fairly obvious, but it is difficult to know what specific moments will generate a response from night to night. Every audience has a unique personality, and you must stay on your toes at all times. This is something that gets easier the longer the run of a show. When there are only a limited number of performances, you need to be especially tuned in to the audience.

When holding for a laugh, you need to keep the moment alive by continuing to respond to the action that got the laugh. Remember not to freeze while the audience laughs, unless it is called for in the action. Don't go on to the next moment until the laughter has reached its peak. You want to be conscientious and caring about your audience, and be sure they don't miss the lines that come directly after the laugh. Some laughs will be quick; others can go on for what seems to be an eternity. Sometimes you may have to actually repeat a line because you came in too early under the laugh. Whatever the case, remember that laughter is infectious, it has the capacity to diffuse and spread. Your ultimate goal is to keep the laughter "rolling."

Early television used "canned laughter," and because it was inserted in a stop–start manner, it sounded abrupt and forced. Once a "studio audience" was introduced into the process with I Love Lucy, the sound of the laughter coming from the television became more natural and less obtrusive to the show. Lucille Ball was especially adept at reading her audience and keeping the moment alive while holding for the laugh. It may be useful to watch some vintage television performances (Dick Van Dyke, Mary Tyler Moore, Lucille Ball) to get a sense of how laughter and timing work in these situations. Shows that are filmed before a live television audience will help you the most.

Holding for applause is similar to holding for the laugh, the two most important rules still apply: you need to hold for the right amount of time, and you need to stay alive while you are holding. This is especially true in a musical; most audiences will applaud at the end of each number. During that applause you need to stay in character and keep the moment alive. Even if you are asked to freeze in position, be careful not to look like a statue. When freezing, keep your eyes alive, hold your position, and don't forget to blink. When you break the applause (just after the crest), stay in character as you move into the next moment. This will help to make the applause feel like it is a necessary and natural part of the action of the show.

Additional Thoughts for the Director

Actors, whether seasoned professionals or enthusiastic amateurs, can benefit from this note sometime during the final technical rehearsals. You might consider discussing it as a group. Ask the actors to share techniques that have worked for them in the past.

Although it is important to anticipate where the audience will laugh or applaud, you cannot completely control their responses. Something that you and the cast found amusing in the rehearsal room could fall flat in front of an audience. Remind the actors to respect the audience rather than blame them for either "not getting the joke" or not applauding in the appropriate place. The last thing you need in performance is an actor at war with his audience. As a director, you might temper your own responses to the material in rehearsal so actors do not learn to expect laughter and overplay the moment.

Other Notes of Interest

> Don't anticipate the laugh.
> Set up the laugh.
> Include the audience.

The Notes

Believability

■ **Note**

Invent the words.

You sound *memorized*.

The Problem

The actor's lines sound rehearsed rather than spontaneous.

Explanation

It is a rare occasion in life when we know precisely what we are going to say next. When we are in a conversation, our minds are fast at work planning possible responses. Sometimes things come out of our mouths that surprise us. Sometimes we struggle to express ourselves and have trouble picking the right words. Sometimes we are inspired and our ideas flow easily. In any case, we listen to what others say and we must come up with our replies on the spot.

Actors need to capture this spontaneity of thought and speech; however, they must do so knowing every word that will be said during the course of the play. They create the illusion that they are composing their thoughts before our eyes and speaking their words for the first time, despite having rehearsed and repeated every moment many times over. A major obstacle for beginning actors, and a constant concern for many with experience, is getting past sounding "memorized" and getting to the point where lines sound fresh and truthful.

Dialogue seems truthful when the audience forgets they are hearing and watching an *actor* reciting lines. This is part of the phenomenon we call "willing suspension of disbelief." The audience believes they are seeing a *character* getting ideas, thinking them through, and inventing lines as she speaks. The character appears to need her words—they become meaningful to her and are essential to expressing her innermost thoughts. Dialogue is less believable when an actor speeds quickly through a speech without taking the time to think as the character or search for any words, such as an actor breezing easily through a Shakespearean monologue without making sense of what she is saying. An awkward line indicates an actor who is uncomfortable or nervous, who has not yet made the lines her own.

Strategies

To make your lines seem more spontaneous, select a passage and go through it slowly, searching for your words. Take each sentence and, as you come across a significant word, pause and go through the following steps:

- Identify the thought you want to express.
- Consider what words might be appropriate.
- Dismiss a few choices.
- Select your word.
- Speak.

Take at least two seconds for each key word. For example, if your line is: "I've always felt close to you," you would say, "I've always felt..." and then pause. Think about your intent—"I want to let her know I have feelings for her, but I don't want to reveal too much." Grapple with how to express this: "I've always felt *friendly*... (no, too cold)... *intimate*... (no, that's too much)... *close*!" Then say your word aloud. The word may come alive for you and have a new emotional resonance. This method will slow you down significantly and become a bit tedious, but it will also get you in touch with the thought process of your character. You will have a stronger commitment to your word choices—you *need* them to express yourself. Once you have done this exercise, you can eliminate the pauses and any "uhs" or "ums" used while searching for your words and then return to your normal pace. You do not want to perform at the slow rate this exercise demands.

Additional Thoughts for the Director

It is important to choose the right time to give this note. When the actors are first off book, they will be struggling with memorization. You need to give them time to get comfortable with their words. But if you wait too long, you risk the words becoming cemented into the actors' learned behavior. The important thing is to reiterate to the actors that their words need to have the necessary "edge" to make them appear as if they are being said for the first time.

Other Notes of Interest

Don't rush.

Earn the pause.

■ Note

Follow your impulse.

Trust your instincts.

The Problem

The actor is blocking creative impulses.

Explanation

We experience impulses every day: "I want to buy that." "I feel like telling her off." "I'm going to ask him out." Some impulses are safe to follow; others involve taking significant risks. We quickly realize that we cannot act on our every urge, so we learn to protect ourselves by monitoring our behavior. When we have a spontaneous idea, we stop before we act, think it over and, more often than not, decide against it.

Whereas impulses in our own lives can lead to trouble, for actors they can lead to more inventive and creative performances. Actor impulses play an important role in character development. Though the basic facts of what a character will say and do are established by the playwright, the nuance and depth of the portrayal—what makes those facts interesting—are left up to the actor. By tapping into the thoughts and instincts of a character, an actor can create a rich and dimensional performance. If an actor follows his impulses, he may come up with new actions, insights, and inflections. His dialogue and physicality may have a greater degree of spontaneity and truthfulness. Though there are many benefits to being open to impulses, some actors overlook them.

Just as we evaluate and discard impulses in our own lives, we do so as actors. Spur-of-the-moment ideas are much riskier than those born out of careful planning. We get an impulse but hold back on it, because we worry it might be inappropriate. We fear looking stupid, making a wrong move, or displeasing the director. We have not learned to trust our instincts.

Sometimes it is obvious when an impulse is being suppressed. For example, when an actor leans at an angle toward the person he is talking to—something you see on stage, but rarely in "real life"—this usually means he has the impulse to take a step but has decided he should not do so. Or an actor who clenches his jaw and bites off his words when his true instinct says to open up his voice and speak passionately. Physical tension is often an indication that an actor has an idea he is afraid to follow.

Strategies

Learning to follow impulses takes some bravery. It is about giving yourself permission to try ideas without evaluating them first, an unnerving thought for those used to being in control. Some spontaneous ideas are bound to be brilliant, while others will fail miserably; but if you put yourself in the shoes of your character your impulses usually will be on the right track. Encourage yourself to experiment with a variety of choices. Setting things too early will often squelch spontaneity.

Improvisational exercises are an excellent means to develop your skill in spontaneity. They demand you think on your feet, give you little time to plan, and no time to worry. They encourage a playful and creative state of mind, which opens the door for impulses to emerge. There are countless improvisational games available, and almost any one of them can prove helpful. A simple character exercise is the hot seat. Ask a scene partner or partners to interview you as your character. Have them ask you questions specific to your scene and more generally about your background and opinions. Have them fire questions to you quickly, and answer each one fully. The interview can move between a friendly dialogue and a confrontational one. This puts you on the spot and requires you to think and respond as your character. You may find that some of your answers surprise you; you may come up with insights you have not thought of before. This exercise can also help you to clarify your character's thoughts and circumstances so you are more open to your impulses.

Additional Thoughts for the Director

Look for moments when an actor is timid with his choices. Perhaps he is either trying an idea but not truly committing to it or starting an action but not following through. This is a signal that he needs some encouragement. Identify his impulse, credit him for it, and give him permission to explore: "It looks like you want to come face to face with your father there; go ahead and try it." Maybe the notion will be terrific and maybe it won't, but by acknowledging the actor's idea and allowing him to pursue it, you will open the door to new impulses and a greater creative collaboration with the actor.

Other Notes of Interest

Take a risk.

You are holding back emotionally.

Raise the stakes.

■ Note

Relate to your character.

Find the humanity in the character.

The Problem

The actor's performance is based on a negative view of the character's situation and actions.

Explanation

While becoming acquainted with a new role, an actor will make many quick decisions about her character. She may subconsciously "type" or categorize elements of the character's personality, or pass judgments on actions and behavior to which she does not immediately relate. These initial impressions can be very strong and hard to shake off. When an actor gives her character a negative label, for example, immature, evil, or stupid, her opinion may cloud her ability to analyze the role. Though playing "evil" may seem enticing and fun, it will lead to a predictable, uninspired performance. Likewise, an overly positive label, such as "saintly," may lead to an actor glossing over some of the character's flaws and foibles.

An actor is the main advocate for her character. She brings the role to life; the voice, body, mind, and heart of the character are channeled through her. If she passes judgment on her character and her prevailing feeling toward her role is negative, this will come through in her portrayal. By feeling superior to the character, an actor distances herself from it and prevents any emotional connection from occurring. The audience sees the actor's *judgment* of the character rather than seeing the character itself. By setting aside prejudices and empathizing with a character, the actor is more likely to create a dimensional, truer-to-the-text portrayal. It is the audience's privilege to view the character within the context of the play and form their own judgments, as the playwright intended.

Strategies

Every character, no matter how strange or contemptible, has some degree of humanity inside. A good approach to finding the sympathetic side to a character is to identify what about her causes your strongest negative reaction. Then determine how the character came to be that way. Question every aspect of her life. Were there traumatic events during childhood? Did she witness something that altered her personality? How was/is she treated by others? What are her inner fears? What has she overcome in her past? What is she protecting herself from? The goal is not to excuse the character from her actions but to understand what led her to make the decisions she did. The script may provide many of the answers, or you may have to use your imagination. Once you can put yourself in the shoes of the character, the role will begin to make more sense.

It is also helpful to find things to like or respect about the character. What does the character love? When is the character honest? What makes her laugh, or cry, or be tender? Sometimes a character may conceal parts of herself; discovering and acknowledging those parts creates a richer picture. Finally, it is important to personally relate to the role you are playing. How are you similar to the character? Find the emotions and experiences you share, even if the character carries them to an extreme beyond your reality.

Additional Thoughts for the Director

No character can be strictly seen as black or white; most of what a character does lies in the shades of gray, giving her actions more depth and complexity. Help the actor to see all the aspects of the character. First, ask her to attack her character's actions and then to defend them. Ask her to imagine what the character's mother or friends think about her. Ask her to compare the character's conscious goals with the thoughts and wishes that may exist on an unconscious level. Coach the actor to invest more in what the character wants overall, her chief desire and goal. The bottom line is to help the actor love playing both the positives and negatives of the character's point of view.

Other Notes of Interest

Find the vulnerability.

Learn to like your role.

With any character, whether they be a villain or a person you want to hate, they are that way for some *reason*. If you come out on stage totally unlikable, and you play the character unlikable, without reason, for two hours, forget about it, you've lost the audience.

—Karen Ziemba

You have to understand how this person ticks. And you can stand and say to anybody, 'Of course I'm liked. This is who I am.' Even if you are playing someone who just killed somebody, you must understand the reason.

—Scott Ellis

■ Note

Concentrate on the action, not on the emotion.

You are playing the character's emotional state.

Your character is covered by an emotional wash.

The Problem

The actor is concentrating only on the emotions of the character leading to a muddy and uncontrolled performance.

Explanation

Emotions are thrilling to play; they feel dramatic and energizing. The emotional state of the character is often easy to identify. An actor will usually sense the emotions of a scene first, before beginning any analysis into his character's actions or motivations. However, emotions can easily overwhelm a scene and cloud an actor's perspective. There are many pitfalls if an actor bases a performance on emotions. Soon all his acting choices become about what he is feeling, while the thought process and actions of the character—the compelling elements—are ignored. As humans we rarely concentrate on creating emotions; rather, emotions appear as we react to our situations. If an actor chooses emotions as a focus, he is not working from a realistic foundation.

This is not to say that characters do not emote; they do. Actors face the challenging task of channeling their characters' emotions in a truthful manner. Actors must learn to open themselves up, to make themselves vulnerable, and to call up reactions and feelings at will. A fine line exists between using an actor's emotions judiciously through the life of a character and indulging them needlessly. Occasionally, moments will click brilliantly, leaving actors elated and convinced that emotions are the key to success. However, more often than not, their emotions will neither appear on cue nor obey the needs and structure of the script. Emotions come in surges. They ignore boundaries, they develop at their own whimsy, and they preempt the actor's thought process. Consequently, performances lose clarity and shape. Audiences are left in confusion and generally unmoved, for they have watched the actor in an emotional state rather than the character in the world of the play.

Strategies

The clearest way to prevent emotions from taking over a scene is to keep your mind centered on the character's actions. Attempting to create emotions is not necessary, for they will arise naturally if you play the given circumstances. The key is to focus on what your character is dealing with, put yourself in his shoes, and tap your imagination to believe in his world. Once you start looking through your character's eyes, you will start feeling what your character is feeling. Analytical work will support this process. Divide your scenes into logical beats or stages, identify your series of actions, and stay focused on your partners' reactions and responses. This technique will help you stay in control of your performance, while giving you the preparation you need for the emotions to surface through the experience of the character. Because the emotion is easy to identify, it is tempting to try to play it immediately. You know what your character should feel, so you want to go for the result as soon as you can. But the best advice is to take it slowly, and not worry about the emotion appearing quickly. The emotion will be more authentic and honest, if you have taken the time to understand the logic of the scene and discovered what triggers it. Patience pays off.

Occasionally, you may find yourself playing a role that is very close to your own life or "close to home." In this case you may find you inadvertently tap into your emotions and are unable to take charge over them. You may want to examine how your character's experience is different from your own and enhance those contrasts. Work imaginatively. Use your scene partners and your objectives to keep your mind focused on the moment at hand; do not let your attention stray. If you are concentrating on specific ideas, actions, or reactions, you are less likely to fall into the trap of indulging your emotions.

Additional Thoughts for the Director

To help an actor focus on the action and not the emotion, refrain from discussing the emotional state of the character as you direct. If a question comes up as to how the character is "feeling" at a particular moment, try to find an active verb that can help the actor shift his thinking off of the emotion and on to the dramatic action. You may also want to run the scene with no emotion whatsoever. Instead, have the actor work specifically on eye contact and clarity of meaning. Is his message being clearly sent and received by the other characters?

Other Notes of Interest

Find the sincerity in an emotional moment.

> You never want to play emotion, that's deadly. DEADLY.
> —Scott Ellis

■ Note

Find the sincerity in an emotional moment.

Play against the emotional cliché.

You are over the top.

The Problem

The actor appears to be straining during a scripted and intensely emotional moment in the action of the play.

Explanation

In our own lives we seldom choose our emotions; they emerge spontaneously from our reactions to our circumstances. When we attempt to make ourselves feel a certain way, we usually fail or end up appearing insincere. Likewise, emotions and attitudes on the stage seem most natural when the actor does not try to force them. There are moments in most dramatic scripts that require the actor to hit a high emotional state on cue. Usually, the story has reached a moment where, for the character, there is a great deal at stake. These kinds of situations require the actor to achieve a specific state reliably from night to night. If the actor places all her concentration and effort into achieving a high emotional state, she will probably come across as false. If she pushes the attitude, she may even seem indulgent or over the top, straining physically and vocally.

When we are in the middle of a strong emotional state, we often strive to suppress it. Think about being in a library and having the urge to laugh. Laughter is not your goal; you know it may cause you to be reprimanded. Instead, you try to keep yourself from laughing, and the harder you try *not* to laugh, the more vigorously the laughter comes. Funerals have a similar effect emotionally. You may feel distraught over the loss of a family member, but you know you need to hold back, if only to show outward strength to your loved ones. The point is that in our own lives we do not think about attaining an emotional response; we often want to fight against it.

Emotions that are out of control can also be difficult for the audience to watch. Actors who strain vocally or physically can often unnerve an audience and make them feel uncomfortable. The struggle to hold back is far more interesting to watch than an emotion that is out of control. Balance is key. The most truthful acting comes when the actor does not worry about *any* emotion, but rather focuses on her actions and lives imaginatively in the world of the play. If she does this, her reactions are honest and fresh from performance to performance.

Strategies

Recreating intense emotional moments on the stage can be tricky. Because forcing the emotion does not work, you must look for another approach. To divert your attention from playing an emotional state, select an action that requires you to fight against it. For example, if your scene involves tears, focus on the need to communicate with your partner. To be understood, you must hold back your sobs, or you may not be able to get your words out at all. You may choose to convince your partner you are feeling fine, and then have to fight the tears so that you can appear composed.

If you have to play a drunken scene, find a reason to stay in charge of your faculties. Prove to others that you are *not* drunk, that the alcohol has not affected you, and that you can do anything you want. The harder you work to demonstrate you are under control, the more believable the drunkenness.

For other states, the process is the same. If you have to be tired, search for an action that will require you to struggle to stay awake. If you are bored, fight to stay involved. If you are angry, work toward controlling your emotions so as not to appear vulnerable. Search for a reason that is appropriate for the scene. Then channel your energy and effort into playing an action that requires you to suppress or control your state of being.

Additional Thoughts for the Director

You will be able to tell if the actor is straining by paying attention to how the scene is being played. Is the actor shouting too much making the words unintelligible and difficult to follow? Is the actor using uncontrolled "fake" laughter? Do the actor's tears appear to be achieved through tension rather than release?

Set up a rehearsal process where the actor is not working only for results but experimenting with different choices and emotional connections. Encourage exploration of opposite behavior and discourage result-oriented acting or overindulgence. If you are having a difficult time convincing the actor to tone it down, have a rehearsal where you break down the scene beat by beat. This will encourage the actor to play the scene from a strong emotional need rather than an emotional result.

Other Notes of Interest

Find the vulnerability.

Control your physical choices.

Concentrate on the action, not on the emotion.

The moment I try to go for an emotional result, tears let's say, nothing happens. I need to go through the building blocks. Plant myself in the reality of the character's circumstance and move chronologically through their time line. If I take every step, I will be delivered to where I need to be emotionally.

—Linda Purl

■ Note

> Make the discovery.
>
> Discover the moment.

The Problem

The actor is not recognizing or reacting to information that is new to the character.

Explanation

Our lives are filled with discoveries. From the trivial—"Oh, I didn't notice I had stained this blouse!"—to the significant, such as finding drugs in a child's room. That moment of discovery, that second when something dawns on us, can transform us and shift our outlook, change our expression, or alter our attitude. We may have a surge of adrenaline. The light bulb is turned on and we suddenly see something in a new way.

Watching a character encounter and respond to new experiences is what makes a play interesting. Discoveries are treasured moments. They move the plot forward and allow the character to learn. When a character makes a discovery, we are immediately drawn into his world. We wonder what will happen next. How will this affect him? What choices will he make? How will the story change?

It is easy for an actor to take new information for granted, either assuming that the character already knew everything or treating the information as "not that important." By not allowing the character to discover and react, the most fascinating moments of the character's journey are removed and the performance is flattened.

Strategies

Discoveries can happen at any point in a scene. They may appear as you walk into a room, as you observe others, or as you react to what is said. They often come to you in the middle of a conversation, as you speak or search for a word. You may have one big discovery or five small ones. Your first step is to identify what discoveries your character makes and when in the scene these occur. Investigation during the script analysis phase of your work will lead you to many of them. However, some of the most interesting discoveries may occur to you during rehearsal, spontaneously, while you are up on your feet and in character. Remain open to new ideas throughout the rehearsal process.

There are many types of discoveries. Some of them are listed in the following:

- discoveries about yourself, such as learning how you really feel, what something means to you, or about your motivations
- discoveries about others, such as their reactions, their intentions, their opinions, their background, their affiliations, their health, or their honesty or dishonesty
- discoveries about your surroundings, such as noticing things and places, seeing something for the first time, or finding changes in familiar items
- discoveries about events and circumstances, such as learning facts about the past or current situation, or hearing about what others are planning or have just done

Once you know your discoveries, you can respond to them. As your character, take in the new information and let it physically affect you. How are you changed? What energy does it give you? What ideas do you get? What decisions do you make? Your response may be subtle or pronounced depending on the situation, but you want to be sure it is shared with the audience so they can experience the discovery with you.

Additional Thoughts for the Director

First discuss with the actor what his character already knows as a scene begins, and then where he discovers new information. Offer suggestions for tactical changes when he is confronted with a discovery. Also, look for the logical shifts in the scene and highlight them with a change in blocking or pace. The most important thing is to instill in the actor a curiosity and desire to continually learn more about the character, the situation, and the story.

Other Notes of Interest

Make the realization.

Make the transition.

Don't anticipate the moment.

■ Note

Don't anticipate the moment.

You are telegraphing.

The Problem

The actor is reacting to something before it has happened, jumping ahead of the immediate moment.

Explanation

Actors have a difficult assignment. Though they know everything that will happen in a scene, as any surprise to the characters is old news to the actors, they must appear as though each moment is occurring for the first time. Sometimes actors will unwittingly give away clues that they are aware of what is to come. They react too early, they physically prepare themselves for a future event, or they signal to the audience they are expecting something. Anticipating will destroy believability and remind the audience they are watching performers and not characters.

For instance, an actor glances at a doorway where someone is about to enter, though her character has no reason to suspect this. Or an actor gets nervous and fidgety moments before the antagonist advances and slaps her in the face. In this case, the actor may be responding on two levels. First, she is anticipating "in character" (she is playing her character's panic too early); second, she is anticipating as an actor (worrying about the stage combat she is going to execute). On both levels she is telegraphing to the audience what is about to happen.

Strategies

The key to avoiding anticipation is to play a scene one moment at a time. Focus fully on what holds the attention of your character at any given point. Listen intently to your scene partners, concentrate on your character's inner thoughts, and do not become distracted by thinking about what is to come. Stay in the present and cope with each new challenge as it arises.

If you find yourself anticipating a major event in a scene, rehearse the scene a few times *without* that event. Stop just before it happens and take some notes. Pinpoint what holds your character's focus, what is on your character's mind at each step, and what your character expects. Then reinsert the missing event while playing your character's moment-to-moment concerns.

Additional Thoughts for the Director

The most effective way to deal with this problem is to work with the actor on pinning down the timing of the moment. Right before the anticipated moment, give the actor a specific thought to focus on that is the direct opposite of what she thinks is about to happen. If you feel that the actor is anticipating an entire *sequence* of events, thus changing the thrust of the scene, help her to clarify *what* is happening *when,* breaking the action down moment by moment. Tell her to come at the scene from a place of innocence rather than of knowledge. This may bring a new dimension to the scene that neither of you anticipated.

Other Notes of Interest

Don't play the ending.

Don't anticipate the laugh.

■ Note

You are working too hard.

You are pushing.

The Problem

The effort of the actor is labored and apparent.

Explanation

An audience wants to "willingly suspend disbelief"—to let go of their hold on reality and to be led into a world of illusion. They want to be absorbed in the lives of the characters and forget for the moment they are watching well-rehearsed actors. When the acting is smooth and confident, the audience feels they are in good hands and they readily give in to the story. If an actor's labors are apparent, the attention of the audience will be directed away from the world of the play and onto the struggles of the actor. This can make the audience uneasy and the production less enjoyable as a whole. Good actors make their craft look easy. The hard work and sweat that goes into the creation of their characters are not visible in their performances.

The job of the actor is a very difficult one. He must transform words on a page into a living, breathing character and do so with ease and grace. Acting often feels like a paradox. The actor analyzes his character so he doesn't have to think about it. He works hard in order to look as if he is not working hard. He focuses intensely on stage, yet relaxes as he does so. It is challenging to find the right balance between effort and release, and actors frequently err on the side of the former.

After all, we have been told for years that if we want to accomplish a goal we have to work hard for it. Achievement-driven personalities thrive on this ethic. If an actor believes a moment in a scene is unsuccessful or uninteresting, he may feel the need to exert more and more effort, hoping that if he only tries harder it will solve the problem. Maybe he feels he is not talented enough for the role and is insecure about what he is doing. The actor concentrates harder, pushes more obviously for his action, and plays his reactions for all they are worth. The result of this is labored, heavy-handed acting—far from the desired effect. Yet this may not stop the actor from continuing to push even more, convinced that trying harder is the only means to a solution.

Another reason an actor may work too hard is he wants to ensure the audience sees all his choices. He may worry they will miss something, so he puts a great deal of effort into each moment to make it clear. He begins to do all the work for the audience, in effect telling them what to think and when. "Look at what I am feeling here. Feel this emotion with me." The actor draws the attention onto himself and what he is doing rather than onto the story. Although his impulse may be to help the audience, he ends up alienating them.

Strategies

If you have done your actor's homework on a scene—that is, if you have carefully analyzed the text, your character, and your actions—then it is time to let it work for you. By preparing your role, you have built a foundation piece by piece, and now you can stand upon that foundation and let it support you. Trust that it is there. It is unnecessary to worry about whether all your insights will be seen and grasped by the audience. Trying to concentrate on a series of individual ideas and pushing each one forward will quickly distort your scene. Your choices will be present without you pointing them out. Trust the audience to make some of the connections for you. At first, it may feel as if you are not doing enough, and by using less effort, your performance will fall flat. Keep your focus on the immediate moment of the scene—what do you need from the other characters? Comfort? Help? Understanding? How are they reacting to you? Put yourself into the mind of the character. What are you thinking? What do you want next? How are you reacting to what you hear? Let the concerns of the character override your urge to worry about whether the audience is "getting" everything you are doing.

If you find it difficult to relax while you are acting, relaxation or meditation exercises before rehearsals and performances may help. A thirty-minute session can be very effective, though you may find that five or ten minutes is long enough to quiet your mind and ready your body. If you allow yourself to slow down, focus your thoughts, and let go of your physical tensions, you will be less likely to feel the need to push.

Additional Thoughts for the Director

Help the actor to trust what he doing is already good; a sincere and sympathetic tone when giving the note will be more effective. Reiterate to the actor his choices are strong and his emotional commitment obvious; now he needs to relax into the moment rather than *acting it out* for the audience. Be sure this note is given about specific moments rather than making a general remark about the actor's entire performance.

Other Notes of Interest

You are thinking too much.

You are monitoring your performance.

You are beating yourself up.

Find the sincerity in an emotional moment.

■ Note

Don't anticipate the laugh.

Don't play for the laugh.

The Problem

The actor is anticipating an audience response to a humorous moment in the play.

Explanation

Getting a laugh can be very tricky. Not only is the technical timing of a joke difficult to achieve, but also humor in general is very subjective. What one audience member finds funny, another may not. How often have you painfully watched as a stand-up comic falls flat or even gets heckled off the stage? Comedy is a tough business.

In a play, some humorous moments will be obvious to the actors and flow naturally; others may be elusive or unpredictable. Of course, every audience is different, made up of individuals who respond in unique ways. Audiences sometimes laugh in places no one anticipated as being funny and, conversely, they sometimes are silent at moments the cast was convinced were hysterical. Laughing is infectious. As the show continues, the audience as a whole begins to take on a collective sense of humor. Usually, the larger the crowd, the bigger and more frequent the laughs.

When an audience is particularly responsive, actors may start to *play* for the laughs rather than continuing to play the action. This means the actors anticipate something funny is approaching and, through their expressions and body language, they communicate to the audience that they want them to laugh. When the actors *tell* the audience how they are to respond, more than likely the audience will not do so.

Strategies

When you play for the laugh you are working on the wrong goal, meaning you are playing an *actor* objective (to get a rise out of the audience) rather than a *character* objective. There may be instances when either a *character* is trying to make another *character* laugh or the dramatic action requires the character to directly address and "amuse the audience" as part of the action, as with many of Shakespeare's clowns and with the use of asides in Restoration comedy. But these are still character, not actor, objectives. If you do your actor homework, then you merely need to concentrate on the action of the scene and trust that the laughs will come forthwith. You must learn to time and perform the joke while paying strict attention to the *character's* objective and not to your own hopes for an audience reaction.

If your timing is forced in rehearsal or you are not getting the desired response in performance, then look to how you are playing the moment. Whatever you do, timing should never look mechanical. It should appear natural to the character, fresh—as if for the first time, and honest—an outgrowth of the dramatic action. Are you physically anticipating the moment? Is it coming out too fast or too slow? Are you ahead of the moment or behind it? Are you vocally anticipating the moment? Do you react with a scream or giggle without truly listening to what is being said? Try to think about why your character is reacting a particular way and add that thinking to your timing.

Comedy needs to appear fresh and honest with each performance. If you think the moment is truly funny, or should be getting a laugh, then it may just be a matter of changing your focus. Try to concentrate on the other characters in the scene. Are you getting the desired response from them? Is your character affected by that response and are you playing it honestly? Try to distinguish between what you and your colleagues found amusing in rehearsal and what is truly humorous about the situation in the script. You may find that what you want the audience to laugh at is more of an "inside" joke between you and the other actors. Because the audience is not privy to the fun you had in rehearsal, the moment will probably go right over their heads.

A lot of failed comedy is a result of actor tension. You may be trying too hard to be funny. This can cause a ripple effect on your whole performance; if you fail to get the first laugh you may try too hard to get the next one. Ultimately, you will only create more tension. To achieve comedy without anticipation, try relaxing into the performance. Free yourself from the goal of trying to get the laugh and let it unfold naturally. You don't want to look as if you are pushing for a reaction because then you will be telegraphing to the audience, "Trust me, this is a funny moment."

Additional Thoughts for the Director

Always useful to a director is Hamlet's Act III, sc. ii, "advice to the players." Specifically about humor, Shakespeare writes: *And let those that play your clowns speak no more than is set down for them: for there be of them that will themselves laugh, to set on some quantity of barren spectators to laugh too; though in the meantime, some necessary question of the play be then to be considered—.* Better advice was never more true than when discussing playing for laughs with your actors. Jokes and funny business are an outgrowth of situation and character. The timing of them is crucial to the telling of the story.

Other Notes of Interest

Connect with your scene partner.

Set up the laugh.

Look for the humor.

If you anticipate or telegraph what's going to happen in a joke, the audience will be way ahead of you. Don't let them get ahead of you.

—Karen Ziemba

■ Note

Commit to the ad lib.

Choose your improvised responses carefully.

The Problem

An actor's improvised lines do not appear natural or motivated.

Explanation

There are many situations that require actors to "ad lib"—to speak improvised lines not written by the playwright. For example, in large group scenes crowd members are often called upon to respond to the action. Whether they are murmurs over a controversial statement or shouts of support and dissent during a debate, these vocalizations can give a scene dimension and add an extra charge of emotion. When actors commit to what they are saying, these group scenes can be realistic and powerful. Sometimes actors, with the knowledge that they are not in focus, resort to saying their lines mechanically and without much conviction. Though the audience may not identify any particular actor in the crowd as being weak, they will perceive the whole as less than effective.

In smaller scenes, it is common to place a couple of people off to the side, deep in discussion, to fill out the stage picture, while other characters are engaged in the main dialogue. In this case, the audience never hears what the actors are saying but should believe they are involved in a realistic conversation pertaining to the action of the play. It is often tempting for actors, because they know they cannot be heard, to talk about things unrelated to the scene, such as how the performance is going or what they are doing after the show. This kind of conversation can only detract from their concentration and from the atmosphere of the scene in general.

Strategies

If you approach your improvisations the way you approach scripted lines, giving them the same time and attention, you will create a rich and detailed performance. Even if your entire role entails being off in a corner in whispered conversation, you can still determine who your character is, what you want at that moment, what drives you, and why you speak. Choose to devise a realistic dialogue rather than "fake" a conversation. The audience can sense when the performers are deeply involved in a play and when they are merely playing the surface of their characters, going through the motions but not believing what they are doing. With your scene partners, work out what topics you'll discuss, who holds which opinions, and what the course of the conversation will be. Without a topic to talk about, it is easy to become distracted and feel awkward or even self-conscious on stage.

If your ad libs are audible, such as when you are playing a member of a crowd, take special care to ensure what you say is appropriate and enhances the dramatic action. Your director may provide you words or phrases to pick from, you may echo what the main characters have stated, or you may choose your own language. Consider the style of the production and the needs of the moment as you select what to say. Ad libs in a Shakespearean play obviously will be of a different nature than those used in a modern one. While the classic phrases of "peas and carrots" and "rhubarb, rhubarb, rhubarb" (traditionally, each member of a group repeats these over and over) successfully create the sound of a noisy crowd, it does not inspire convincing characterizations. You want your words to be specific to the moment, motivated, and truthful.

Additional Thoughts for the Director

The most important measure you can take to ensure ad libs are authentic is to allot rehearsal time for them, rather than assuming they will take care of themselves. Stress the necessity and importance of "whispered conversations" and talk about the effect they generate in the scene. If you have a large-scale scene that demands a number of specific reactions, take time to orchestrate all the crowd responses. Many scenes of this magnitude are usually centered on a debate over one particular issue. Make sure each participant knows which side of the debate he is on and whether his opinion changes during the course of the scene. If you are rehearsing a style or period piece, you and the cast may want to take time to generate a list of ad libs appropriate to the play.

Other Notes of Interest

Give focus/take focus.

■ Note

    Tone down your expressions.

    You are indicating.

    You are mugging.

The Problem

The actor's facial expressions are exaggerated and appear untruthful.

Explanation

Creating a clear and truthful performance is one of the most difficult challenges an actor has to face. Occasionally an actor, intending to be especially clear, overplays reactions without knowing it, trying to show what the character is feeling at each moment. The actor's concentration is centered on whether the audience is "getting" what she is doing, which leads her to use broad facial expressions as she reacts to events on stage. "See, I'm surprised at what he said. Now I'm puzzled about what to do next." Though the actor is clearly communicating how the character is reacting, she is not believable. The audience is aware they are watching an actor "acting" rather than being drawn in by a character responding in the moment. The actor's work, in this case, is seen primarily on her face. She acts from the neck up and the rest of the body is not connected to her responses.

Strategies

One of the best strategies for this problem is to strengthen your inner monologue. Throw your full focus into what is on your character's mind: what she wants from the other character, what she is thinking, and what she is experiencing. Keep your concentration on the present moment, the other character, and on what is going on in your character's life. You do not need to concern yourself with *showing* the audience what is on your mind. All you have to do is *think as the character*, and the audience will understand. This will feel like a lot less effort, and it is. You are allowing the audience to do some of the work for you.

We are often surprised by how big our reactions look in a photograph or on video. "Was I really that exaggerated?" "Did I really look that unrealistic?" You may find it helpful to work briefly with a hand mirror. Rehearse a portion of a scene on your own, and at key moments hold up the mirror to make note of your expression. Is it exaggerated? Do you have a lot of tension in your face? Can you relax your muscles? Once you have a sense of what you are doing, put the mirror away. Though it may be tempting to practice expressions in the mirror, the spontaneity and truthfulness you are aiming for are best achieved without thinking about how you look.

Additional Thoughts for the Director

Remind the actors that the mask of a character is not just the face, but the entire body. Neutral masks can be a very useful rehearsal technique to ensure complete physical involvement. In a two-person scene, have the actors play the scene, one in mask (she will not be able to speak) and the other unmasked (he will be speaking only his lines). Coach the masked actor to drop her facial expressions down into her center as she responds to the actor speaking the text. When she feels the urge to "reply" by moving her head and shoulders in agreement or disagreement, challenge her to drop those expressions down into her body. Now reverse the actor positions and play the scene again. Try the scene one more time with both actors masked. Coach them through the beats of the scene and have them only respond physically. Finally, play the scene without masks. This exercise will also help you to strengthen the listening and responding from each actor in the scene.

Other Notes of Interest

> You are thinking too much.
>
> You are working too hard.
>
> I would have a lot of trouble giving the note 'You are mugging' because I feel like it's negative. And then the actor tries <u>not</u> to mug. I'd say, 'Relax your face more,' or 'Let the character wear more of a mask, so that what's going on, all the changes the character is experiencing, we don't see so clearly.'
>
> —Bill Rauch

■ Note

> Know the world of the play.
>
> Embrace the style of production.
>
> Know what kind of play you are in.

The Problem

The actor's behavior as the character is inconsistent with the given circumstances of the play and/or style of the production.

Explanation

Ninety percent of theatre produced by schools, regional theatres, and even Broadway is a revival of a tried and true text. While the theatre today is alive with playwrights writing new works set in contemporary times, most of what the actor will encounter in a career in the theatre are reinvented productions of classics, period plays, and musicals. In addition, many new plays are set in earlier eras, for example, Tom Stoppard's *Arcadia* or Peter Shaffer's *Amadeus*. Plays from other countries have also been translated for an English-speaking audience. Every play is written for a specific time and audience, in response to specific events, from a playwright who lived in a specific world. A director may wish to keep a play in the time and place in which it was written, to highlight only certain aspects of that period, or to place it in an entirely different period. Style for the theatre is created through the imagination of the director and designers of the play as they interpret the text for a contemporary audience. In any case, it is crucial for the actor to have a clear understanding of the world of the play and of the era the production will be set. There can be a myriad of different ways of producing the same play.

Actors unschooled in the rich and varied history of the theatre can sometimes have difficulty embracing the world of the play. This problem is usually manifested in the physical and vocal life of the actor's portrayal; that is, the character looks and sounds too contemporary. We are all products of our own time. We all have our own "style" as individuals; the things we choose to wear, the language we choose to use, and the way we choose to move are all part of the presentation of ourselves as unique individuals or members of a group. Likewise, each character reflects the time and place in which he lives. Discovering and embodying this information is part of the actor's craft.

Strategies

The great actor Sir John Gielgud is often quoted as having said, "Style is knowing what kind of play you are in." This means you need to embrace all the given circumstances of the play as written by the playwright. The year, date, time, and place all influence the playing style for the actors. A strong understanding of the given circumstances, including the social, economic, political, and religious environments can be an invaluable fount of information for an actor. Whatever the production concept, some information does not change from production to production. The status and relationships of the characters must be acknowledged in some manner. No matter what the style, Hamlet is still a "prince" of sorts, his father has been murdered and his uncle is the current "head of household" married to his mother the "queen." Clarify the information about your character given in the text:

- class distinction: upper, middle, lower, servant, etc.
- education and background

- economic situation: rich, comfortable, poor, destitute, etc.
- political views
- religious views

There are many dramaturgical resources available to heighten your awareness of the given circumstances of a play: watch movies and videos filmed in a similar period, study the artwork of the times, or read books on manners of the day. If you concentrate on achieving accurate period manners and movement you may appear stiff and lifeless, as though you were performing in a museum piece, or as Peter Brook terms it "The Deadly Theatre." Remember to connect all decisions on manners and movement to your overall objective as a character.

Clothing affects many things: how you move, how you behave, how you choose to be perceived by others. This is called your character's decorum. Because you will not be in your costume until the technical rehearsals, using rehearsal clothing can be extremely valuable to your artistic process. It is said that Sir Lawrence Olivier would not begin rehearsals until he was given the shoes he would be performing in. While you may not have this luxury, you can ask for specific pieces of clothing, such as a corset, cape, or cloak to work in. Or you can bring a substitute from your wardrobe at home. If you are wearing a coat of some kind in the scene, do not just rehearse in a tee shirt. If you are wearing formal shoes, do not rehearse in sneakers.

Finally, finding the vocal life of your character will also help you to look and feel the part. Examine your text for clues as to how your character speaks. Are there words, phrases, or sentence patterns your character uses that you would not use in your own daily speech? How do you address others? Formally ("sir" or "madam") or informally ("sweetie" or "dear")? If you were to consider your text as a piece of music, how would it be played? Flowing or staccato? Quickly or slowly? Listen to the variety of pitches or the symphony of sounds created by the other actors and find your voice in that world.

Additional Thoughts for the Director

Everyone in rehearsal should be focused on extraordinary unity of purpose and playing, with characters living together in a unified and consistent world. Be specific about what you want the show to look and feel like. Help the actors to be on the same page physically and vocally, by setting specific parameters for the production. Clarify what is important to you about the style and continue to relay this information throughout the rehearsal process. Present your research and the research of the designers in actable, tangible terms. Sharing selected music, photographs, paintings, recordings, or quotes may be useful. Try not to overwhelm them with too much information all at once. Sort out what the actors need to know to make the style work for your audience. You may also want to give the actors either a style "cheat sheet" or an actor "check-list" that highlights all the information you have been rehearsing with them, again in simple, actable terms.

Other Notes of Interest

Relate to your character.

> Manners are not 'mannered.' Look for the reasons behind the manners: they were clothed differently, there were different expectations.
>
> —Scott Ellis

Rehearsal Problems

■ Note

You are setting choices too early.

Remain open to the rehearsal process.

The Problem

The actor is locking into a performance early in the rehearsal process.

Explanation

Rehearsal periods can vary greatly in length, from one week to several months. There is a unique rhythm to every rehearsal. Usually there is time for actors to explore choices, for lines to be mastered, for scenes to be deepened, and for the play to be polished. In a short rehearsal period, these stages happen very quickly; in a longer process, each step can afford more time. It is important for actors to pace themselves according to the allotted time, not lingering too long in the initial explorations nor rushing too quickly to the final polishing.

In some cases, the audition process can work against this. A director may ask the actors to prove they can pull off a particularly challenging role by attempting full performance levels during the readings. When rehearsals begin, it can be hard to let go of the choices and the performance energy found in the auditions. Occasionally, actors close themselves off from any idea that did not occur to them while they were vying for their parts.

Some actors habitually strive to get to the end product as quickly as possible. For them, the exploratory period feels uncomfortable and unsettling. In an effort to get a strong handle on their roles, they latch onto their first impressions or employ ideas that have worked for them in the past. Once they have decided how they are going to play a scene, they are reluctant to change, fearful new ideas will not be as strong.

In any of the previous cases, actors are working against the rhythm of the rehearsal process, by setting choices too early, and not fully exploring their characters. The consequences for an actor can include losing interest in the role, locking into choices before fully understanding the play, or becoming stale and forced.

Strategies

If you find it difficult to let go of choices you've made early in the rehearsal process, try experimenting *around* those choices. This can be done as you practice on your own, or with the director's consent, during rehearsal. Take your basic actions and interpretations and vary how you enact them. For instance, approach them in a lighter manner; this could mean being more playful, more vulnerable, or anywhere in between. Run through the scene twice in this way, and note any discoveries you have made. Then return to your original approach for one time through. Then for the next two runs, vary in the opposite manner, for instance, with a strong hand, with more intensity, or more conviction. Again, return to your original approach. Afterward, compare the three approaches and examine your reactions. Did some of your original ideas seem less effective after your experimentation? Did you gain insight into how to make a certain moment better? Did you open your mind to new possibilities?

Additional Thoughts for the Director

Remember, an actor's instinct is a very powerful tool to be encouraged in the rehearsal process. Their initial response to the material is usually accurate. It is crucial to create an environment where it is okay to fail, so actors feel comfortable experimenting with their choices. They may indeed come back to their initial response to the material, but rehearsal exploration will make that initial response richer and deeper, more complex, and ultimately easier and more reliable to find every performance.

Other Notes of Interest

Look for the opposite.

Use more variety in your choices.

Go back to your script.

I find it crucial to honor the process and not stress for result in the early days. In other words, to trust both the failures and successes within the rehearsal process.

—Linda Purl

■ Note

Do your homework.

Bring something new into rehearsal.

The Problem

The actor is only working on his role during scheduled rehearsals.

Explanation

The term rehearsal comes from *rehercier* meaning to harrow the soil. When the soil is turned again and again, it becomes more fertile. Likewise, during rehearsal, the ideas in the script are lifted and turned while the actors and director dig to find meaning. The more exploration that occurs, the more productive the process. An important part of the actor's job is to continue to dig and explore between rehearsals to ensure the process as a whole is as rich as possible.

A mistake some actors make is to assume their homework merely consists of memorizing their lines. Though memorization is a crucial task done outside the rehearsal room, it is only the beginning of the actor's discipline. Ideally, an actor's performance grows between rehearsals. An actor should not only review and reinforce what he has learned at a rehearsal but also investigate his role in further depth. This way, when he returns to the next rehearsal, he is better prepared and ready to take a step forward. An actor who is continually thinking through his role and working out details on his own will be more productive in rehearsal. Actors who use their outside time solely for memorization often return to rehearsal having forgotten what they did the day before, and precious rehearsal is wasted rehashing the same material. This slows down progress for everyone and can adversely affect the play as a whole.

Of course, it is easier to be disciplined and diligent in a formal rehearsal situation than it is when sitting alone at home. However, serious actors will see rehearsal time with the director and cast as only half of their work. Many important elements, such as understanding the role, getting into the skin of the character, making sense of the character's thought process, and getting words and movements to become second nature, come together during private rehearsal, when an actor can concentrate on the details of his performance.

Strategies

Motivation, discipline, and organization of time are the keys to your success. First comes motivation. Find something in the role that intrigues or challenges you as an artist. What skills can you hone with this role? How can you refine your rehearsal process? If the performance is important to you, you will invest more energy into your work. Next comes discipline. A good musician will spend hours in the practice room learning notes, working out fingering, going repeatedly over a difficult movement, and thinking about the thematic structure and dynamics of the music. Just so, actors need concentrated time for vocal and physical warm-ups, script work, and individual rehearsal. Discipline takes dedication, daily effort, and a focused work ethic.

Finally comes the most difficult task, organizing your time. Because rehearsals often take large portions of your day and other responsibilities battle for the rest of your time, it is a challenge to find space in your schedule. Establishing a routine can help. Find a time and place clear from other distractions. Make your private work a priority.

In the first stages of working on your role, it is a good idea to spend time reading your script over and over, searching for clues about your character. Keep a notebook and record your impressions. Also look for specific answers to the following questions:

- What notes or stage directions does the playwright provide regarding your character?
- What does your character say about himself? How does he feel about himself?
- What do the other characters say about him? How do they feel about him?
- What insights do you have into your character's history?

- What is revealed about your character through his behavior?
- What is the central objective of your character?

As you study, you will come up with your own questions, ideas, insights, as well as confusions and uncertainties about specific moments. Bring these to rehearsal. A good director appreciates an actor who comes in with an idea to try or a question to discuss.

Beyond script analysis, you also want to get on your feet and work. Review new choices which were made in your last rehearsal. Perhaps the director has given you a note you need to work on, or there is a moment you are having trouble with that needs some exploration. There are countless aspects to a role that may demand your attention, for example, trying different actions, working out transitions, discovering motivations, physicalizing your character, drilling a dialect, working with a difficult prop or costume piece, or practicing a dance routine. Experiment with ideas, refine choices, and dig deeper into your role. If you do not know what element of your performance to work on, ask your director for guidance.

Additional Thoughts for the Director

At the end of each rehearsal, take a few moments to ask the actors what they feel they need to work on outside of rehearsal. Offer a few suggestions such as "try experimenting with your objective in the scene," or "work on scoring that moment until it feels comfortable." Make sure you are not doing all the homework for them. Ask the actors questions rather than offering the only solution. By inspiring the actors to think outside rehearsal, and to bring something new in each time, you will empower them to be more collaborative during the process.

Other Notes of Interest

Learn to like your role.

Go back to your script.

Make the blocking your own.

■ Note

Go back to your script.

The Problem

The actor needs to reread the script for one or more of the following reasons: to check for accuracy in memorization, to strengthen the connection with the character, or to gain a fresh perspective on the script as a whole.

Explanation

A director will often suggest to the cast to "go back to the script" at the latter stages of the rehearsal process. The initial script study serves as the foundation for the final stages of work and is crucial in equipping actors with the information and background necessary for fully interpreting and realizing their roles. When actors start to prepare for roles, scripts are rarely far from their hands. Studying lines, subtext, character traits, and relationships is a central concern, and actors will dedicate much of their time to this task. As the lines are learned, the blocking is solidified, and run-throughs begin, actors tend to limit their script study to their most difficult passages. They do not spend as much concentrated effort on reading the script as a whole. Once the play is up on its feet, the preliminary homework is laid aside and script study is replaced by questions of timing, flow, and polishing.

The focus of the actor's concentration is different from the beginning to the end of the rehearsal process. An actor should not be spending as much time with the script on the last week of rehearsal as during the first week. However, it is often very useful to go back to the script once the play is in run-throughs to reconnect with earlier discoveries which may have been forgotten or ignored. Of course, as actors grow with a character, their view and interpretations change from those they held when they started. But by looking back at the script, actors may find new connections and insights into their work. A new idea may surface, perhaps regarding the meaning of a line or how to motivate it, or an old idea may resurface and prove useful. Both have the potential to enrich an actor's performance. Sometimes a small, subtle change will be the result; other times a significant realization will boldly shape the actor's characterization. Because the script is the origin of all the work, it pays to keep going back to it throughout the rehearsal process.

Another interesting discovery occurs with reviewing lines. After being off-book for awhile, actors tend to develop their own "versions" of some of their lines. Slight paraphrasing or reordering of lines is frequent and often happens without actors realizing that they are doing so. By going back to the script and rereading their lines carefully, they will often discover changes they have made that alter the original idea of the playwright. A replaced word, an omission, or a switched line can deprive a speech of some of its power and effectiveness. By restoring the playwright's words, an actor is often able to get a new grasp on a line or a renewed understanding of its meaning.

Strategies

Going back to the script involves more than rereading lines. You will discover if you just open your script and start reading, you will only find what you already know. Your eye may automatically jump to your cue lines or what you have highlighted on the page. Allow time to really absorb what you are reading and to dwell on pages without feeling rushed to finish. Find a room, preferably away from the theatre, where you will not be disturbed and where you can relax comfortably. You may want to get a clean copy of the script, without your blocking or notes in the margin. Imagine you are picking up a play you have never read, and try to start with a clear mind. Let the words and plot be a surprise to you; avoid visualizing the actors and the staging of the particular production you are in. You want to see the characters as the playwright wrote them. As you read, it may help to keep a notebook nearby to write down your impressions, conclusions, and discoveries. Make note of the lines which may have new meaning for you, and the lines which you have memorized incorrectly. When you have altered lines, ask yourself if the *real* words offer clues to your character's thought process. A simple revisiting of the text can crystallize many aspects of your performance and reconnect you to your original instincts about your character.

Additional Thoughts for the Director

This is a good note to give when you are in the final stages of rehearsal, preferably just before technical and dress rehearsals. The actors are about to confront new aspects of the production and they need to refresh themselves and renew their excitement about the play. Ask the company to think as an audience member would upon hearing the lines for the first time. Encourage them to read the entire play to appreciate both the story as a whole and the various characters as unique individuals. Save time during note sessions to have a discussion about the play, as you did when you first started your table work. As a group, reacquaint each other with the reasons you found the play interesting and worthy of producing.

Other Notes of Interest

Tell the story.

Trust the text.

When I feel lost I go back and quietly, slowly reread the play.
—Linda Purl

■ Note

Invest energy into the rehearsal.

Don't save it for the audience.

The Problem

The actor is not investing any energy or connecting emotionally to the role during rehearsals.

Explanation

Some actors only come alive when they are in front of an audience. When they feel the energy and hear responses coming from the house, their adrenaline begins to flow and they attack their roles with gusto. This can be a magical sensation and leave actors feeling invigorated and successful. Some actors are able to pull this technique off; their performances seem spontaneous and fresh, and their characterizations fall into place. However, this approach is not without many pitfalls. Untested energy and commitment can result in occasional rash choices, overplaying moments, and catching other actors off guard. To rely on this extra kick of energy to shape an entire performance is unwise and can also affect the rest of the ensemble. The director is unable to get an accurate impression of how performances will interrelate and balance one another and must rely on guesswork when trying to coach and guide the actors. The opportunity for trial and error and refining choices is lost, and the director can only plant seeds in an actor's mind and trust he will act on them in performance.

An actor who tends to hold back energy may rehearse his lines with no expression while inwardly planning his performance. This makes it difficult for fellow actors because they have nothing to respond to and therefore cannot gauge how much effort they will need to use. They may compensate by either raising their own energy level several notches or trying to engage the other actor's interest. This can begin to distort their performances as they push more and more. They may find their commitment waning as well, that the other actor's lack of expression is contagious and is pulling them down. In either case, they are left with questions such as: "What will the actor do in performance?" "How is the actor going to play that moment?" "What should we expect and how should we prepare?" The cast may begin to worry the actor is not going to come through at all, and the play as a whole will suffer.

Strategies

You may fear that rehearsing at full power will deplete your resources and cause actor "burn out" before you open the show. Pacing yourself is important and you should be sensitive to when you are losing interest in a scene or when your energy is dwindling. However, if you always pull back, you deprive yourself and those around you the chance to see how the scene will really play in performance. When you are in character and fully committed, you can make discoveries and connect to emotions. This needs to happen in the rehearsal room. Conserve your energy when you are offstage and during breaks. When you are on stage, treat your director, stage manager, and fellow actors as your audience, giving you a reason to be "up." If on a particular day you feel the need to reserve energy, let the director and other actors know. Ask the director to tell you when it is important to see your performance at full intensity during the rehearsal period, and agree to do so. A little negotiation may satisfy everyone's needs.

You may encounter circumstances where you don't want to hold back very often, such as with a very challenging role that requires a lot of stamina. You may decide you need the time in rehearsal to build vocal and physical strength and to prepare yourself for the rigors of performance. You will never lose that extra layer of excitement and anticipation that the actual performance brings. Knowing there is an audience inevitably deepens and energizes your work, but you will be more prepared for this change if you commit fully to what you are doing in rehearsals.

There may be special circumstances when you do not want to fully realize a moment during every rehearsal. Certain roles may demand extraordinary emotional commitment; certain moments may be very delicate and fragile. To rehearse at performance energy too early or too frequently could risk exhausting your stamina or drying up your emotional reserve. In these types of scenes, it would be acceptable to save fuel for the performances and to hold back during certain rehearsals. However, this should be a mutually understood and agreed upon decision. There will be a few strategically timed rehearsals where you would want to have a dry run at performance energy to determine the effectiveness of choices and to become aware of what will be demanded.

Additional Thoughts for the Director

This problem is a more common occurrence than one might think. Talk to the actor privately rather than risk embarrassing him in front of other cast members. Have a serious heart-to-heart discussion, reassuring him that you feel he is capable of handling the role, but you have yet to see him commit fully and invest all his energy into the performance. Perhaps he will have a concern you can work out together. If he doesn't think there is a problem, don't push the issue at that moment. You may find that just talking to the actor will be enough for him to make a change.

Other Notes of Interest

You are holding back emotionally.

> The rehearsal is the most important process. You never get it back. It's the only time you really have the freedom to explore and fail, because once you get in front of an audience you tend to not want to do that. You protect yourself. So it's very important you be in the moment during rehearsals and allow yourself to rehearse.
>
> —Scott Ellis

■ Note

Learn to like your role.

Find the challenges in the role.

The Problem

The actor has a negative attitude toward the role, which is interfering with the rehearsal process.

Explanation

Actors often have little control over how they are cast. This can inevitably cause tension, especially when some actors discover they are not assigned the part they desired. While actors with leading roles are usually the happiest, actors in smaller or unglamorous parts may be less than enthusiastic. Complaints may range from "The role is too small to be worth my time," to "I don't get to do anything in this part; it is just a 'function' character." Dissatisfaction with casting is not limited to students and amateurs. It is not uncommon to hear of professional repertory actors bargaining with producers for roles, "If I can have the 'juicy part' in Script X, I'll play the cameo for you in Script Y." Of course, every role must be filled for a play to be produced and, ideally, filled with a strong performer. When actors are disgruntled with their roles, they are less likely to be fully committed in rehearsals and performance.

Strategies

You probably wish every role you play could be exciting and interesting. When this is not the case, you must work to find something in the role to engage your attention and keep you motivated. Once you have a constructive attitude, you will see that almost every part offers the chance to create a vivid and memorable characterization.

One of the simplest methods to keep yourself feeling challenged is to consciously use your role as an opportunity to refine your craft. Select one or more skills you want to deepen and improve. Focus on these elements as you rehearse, giving attention to both the demands of the role and the enrichment of your skills. The list of acting topics is endless; a few possible choices are included in the following:

- timing
- physical characterization
- focus
- breath
- vocal resonance
- developing a character biography
- spontaneity/being in the moment

We all have heard of the actor in a cameo role who "stole the show." Though stealing the spotlight should never be the goal, it is clear roles of all sizes and types can make striking impressions on the audience. Relieved of the pressure to carry the show, and afforded the luxury of time to focus on details of your performance, you can expend more energy on developing the depth and subtlety of your character. In addition, usually you have more time to appreciate the process and to enjoy your colleagues. Finding the right attitude, moving from resenting a role, to seeing it as a useful opportunity, can make a significant difference.

Additional Thoughts for the Director

As directors, we spend a great deal of time working with the leading characters, and sometimes can abandon the actors playing the smaller roles. Take time in rehearsal to make sure all the actors are feeling their roles are important to the play. Allow them time to experiment with their character choices, appearance, and decorum; give them the freedom to create something they can be proud to play. Be sure to give these actors notes, even when you are busy and focused on the major characters. Actors who never receive notes or guidance from the director quickly conclude they are insignificant. Remind them that the smaller roles create the foundation of the play.

Other Notes of Interest

Leave your personal problems outside the rehearsal space.

> I think to some degree you fall in love with every character you portray because you come to know them so intimately.
>
> —Linda Purl

■ Note

> You are beating yourself up.
> You are being too hard on yourself.

The Problem

The actor is overly self-critical.

Explanation

Most serious actors set high standards for themselves, aiming for the best possible performance. Also, most actors have doubts, be they momentary or long term, about their abilities to achieve these goals. Even award-winning actors have been known to quake backstage, unsure of their capacity to perform. Some actors either lack confidence in themselves or fear others think them to be inadequate. Some are "pleasers" looking for the approval of their director, fellow actors, and the audience. One of the challenges actors face is being able to maintain their concentration in the midst of these self-doubts and fears.

Actors who are self-critical tend to work hard and have the best of intentions, but their worries create a constant state of tension. As they rehearse, each of their mistakes, such as a missed line or a less-than-perfect moment, becomes a reason to flinch or be dissatisfied. Nothing slips by them. Sometimes actors will stop midscene to apologize, to put themselves down, or to let others know they were not satisfied. Of course, this behavior breaks the flow of the rehearsal and frustrates everyone involved. Other actors may save their dismay to the end of a scene, when they express their unhappiness, curse, or go into a quiet depression. Note sessions can be traumatic for these actors, as they often interpret their director's comments as criticism, further confirmation that they are not doing well and that their performance is deficient.

Strategies

If you are in the habit of berating yourself, you probably spend a lot of time worrying about the quality of your performance. Will you be able to pull it off? Why aren't you doing everything right? Are you good enough? Focusing on these issues means you care about your work, a commendable trait. However, anguishing over your abilities wastes your energy, energy that you could channel into bettering your performance.

Erasing negative thoughts is not always possible. Rather than trying to rid yourself of self-criticism, give yourself a specific task to focus on. Identify one thing you want to work on in your performance. Once you have addressed that, move onto the next item. Taking it step by step helps you to concentrate and gives you reasonable, attainable goals. When you worry about your entire performance and try to fix everything at once, it is easy to feel overwhelmed and inadequate.

As you perform, anchor your mind on your character's moment-to-moment thoughts and desires. If you find you are thinking about how well you are doing, or you have the urge to stop and complain about a mistake, use this as a trigger to strengthen your focus on your character. If you become frustrated with yourself, use this surge of energy to enhance what you are doing; let the frustration become determination to stay focused.

When a director gives you notes, remember this is an essential part of the collaboration between artists. Because you are unable to watch your own performance, you rely on the eye of the director to give you feedback and suggestions. A note means a director believes you have the ability to improve, and he finds it worthwhile to help you. It means the director cares about how you are doing and wants you to give your best performance. When notes are seen as friendly support rather than as criticism, you will be more able to relax and receive them.

Additional Thoughts for the Director

Reiterate to the actor your belief in what he is doing. Reassure him that he was cast for very specific reasons and highlight those reasons in his mind. After all, if you did not believe in his ability to succeed, you would not have given him the part. Remind him there is much about himself as a person he can offer to the playing of the role. If you notice the actor appears to be insecure, first praise him for what he is doing well and then offer specific suggestions for improvements. These tactics will aid the actor toward positive rather than negative and unproductive thinking.

Other Notes of Interest

You are monitoring your performance.

■ Note

Leave personal problems outside the rehearsal space.

Keep a professional attitude.

Concentrate on rehearsing.

The Problem

The actor's attitude and/or personal problems are infringing on the rehearsal process.

Explanation

Rehearsal taxes you mentally, physically, and emotionally. It requires tremendous concentration and an extended attention span. These demands can be invigorating and motivating when you are feeling up to the task, but when your energy is low, they can be overwhelming. When an actor has a bad day or is feeling sick or tired, it is especially difficult to generate the energy necessary to make it through rehearsal.

Everyone has occasions when they are faced with personal challenges, whether they be family or relationship difficulties, money struggles, or bad news. These problems cannot be solved in the rehearsal room, but if unchecked, they can become major distractions. If an actor dwells on personal issues, her focus is divided and therefore she is unable to keep her full concentration on rehearsing. Learning to leave problems at the door is not easy, but it is an important part of the actor's job.

Issues within the rehearsal room can also interfere with an actor's concentration. There may be either a particular cast member that gets on everyone's nerves or a director who does not listen to the ideas of the actors. The cast may be forming cliques, causing some people to feel excluded or unwelcome. Sometimes a moment in the play hits a particularly raw nerve and an actor gets a little oversensitized. Keeping a professional attitude and staying focused on the work helps an actor navigate through tense rehearsals.

Strategies

Though it is hard to simply "set aside" problems or complaints, it can benefit you in the long run. By throwing yourself into rehearsal, you gain a few hours of respite and relief from your worries. Staying focused on a task helps to keep you from dwelling on negative thoughts and gives you a fresh perspective on personal matters when you have to return to them. There are many things you can do to prepare yourself mentally and physically for rehearsal.

- Exercise or take a walk to get your heart pumping and to clear your mind.
- Listen to energizing music on the way to rehearsal. Bring headphones to listen to music during breaks.
- Set aside time to do a thorough warm-up, giving special attention to centering your thoughts.
- Arrive early to rehearsal to allow yourself time to focus on your role.
- Ask another actor to meet you to run lines.

If you are seriously ill or contagious, of course you will need to stay home. Otherwise, make the effort to come to rehearsal. Working on the role may take your mind off feeling miserable. Remember that complaining about minor aches and pains, especially about being tired, may mean you are avoiding a more serious problem in your work.

When tensions develop between people in the rehearsal room, this can lead to stressful working relationships and negative attitudes. As you confront this type of situation, ask yourself: "What is in the best interest of the play?" "Can I let a negative comment roll off my back?" Keep your focus on rehearsal and off behind-the-scenes battles. If tensions grow, you may need to take a colleague aside and talk things out privately. Just as you select objectives for your characters, you may want to pick an objective for yourself to help you through a difficult rehearsal. Try "to cooperate," "to keep an open mind," or some other positive statement you find helpful.

Perhaps you find yourself resistant, anxious, or defensive during rehearsals, but you are unable to blame your mood on either outside events or on how you are treated by others. Ask yourself if you have fears about your role. Are you insecure or overwhelmed by its challenges? Does the role deal with a subject matter you are sensitive to? If you discover this to be the case, discuss your reactions either with your director or with someone you can trust. Confronting your fears is the healthiest way to overcoming them.

Additional Thoughts for the Director

Just as the actors need to leave their day outside, so too does the director. The actors take their cue from your physical presence and energy. If you appear tired or upset, they will take this to mean they have the liberty to do the same. When you enter the rehearsal room, maintain an air of professionalism. Once you start, try to create an environment where work is the primary objective. Set goals for each of your rehearsals to keep the process moving forward. Create an atmosphere of collaboration by investing in the creativity of your actors. Moments of inspiration often come from something the actor is already doing. Pay attention to what they are giving you and help them to clarify their intentions.

The director also needs to be aware when the tensions in the room are high. If the rehearsal seems to be straying from the work at hand, try conducting an improvisation around the moment or scene. If this does not work, take a break or leave the scene you are working on for a later rehearsal to come back to it with a fresh perspective.

A pet peeve of most directors is actors who chat on the sidelines when not directly involved in the scene. If this is a problem, ask the stage manager to gently remind the actors to keep focused on the rehearsal. If they want to chat or work on a different part of the play, have them do so outside the room. If you have an actor who is being especially difficult, it is always a good idea to have a private talk. A one-on-one conversation, rather than a public debate, can be especially fruitful for both the director and the actor.

Other Notes of Interest

Invest energy into the rehearsal.

> Never be sick or tired. I don't care if an actor is sick or tired, come
> in and do your work. Keep personal problems outside. You've got to
> close the door. Put it away and close the door.
>
> —Scott Ellis

> The work space is sacred, it must be honored. It mustn't be polluted.
>
> —Linda Purl

Moving into the Theatre

Near the end of the rehearsal process, one of the most difficult transitions for the actors and director is the move from the rehearsal room into the theatre. It is crucial for the director to build transfer time into the rehearsal schedule, as the actors need to make a number of mental, physical, and vocal adjustments before the technical and dress rehearsals can begin. The set will probably be unfinished, but even a skeletal structure (platforms, entrances, exits, perhaps the actual furniture) is enough to make the rehearsals productive.

Moving into the theatre can be a very exciting, though occasionally frustrating time for all involved. Even if you have worked in a particular space before, you need to approach it as if for the first time. Each play has a different "feel"; each world is unique. There will be many physical and vocal demands placed on the actor that are special to that particular play. What you did in the rehearsal room will change. Go into the rehearsals in the theatre with an open mind. Be ready to adjust your choices to fit the new environment.

Rehearsal rooms are usually very small and intimate. There is often only enough space to tape out the stage, leaving just a modest area from which the stage management and directorial staff must work. This can be very unnerving for the actors at first. Everyone is in such close proximity to the action that you can almost hear one another breathe. This kind of intimacy can be useful in the early stages of rehearsal. You can respond very quickly to a director's physical and vocal communications. You can look for approval or disapproval in what you have chosen to do. Other cast members are usually present to offer support, watch the flow of the play, and study the other characters. Sometimes the rehearsal room is like a womb, feeding and nurturing your performance until it is ready to be seen in public. Many actors *love* to rehearse and *hate* to move out of this womblike environment. For them, they may rely on this kind of intimacy as a security blanket. Others can hardly wait to be on the stage and eventually get to "play" in front of a real audience. Whatever kind of actor you are, the move to the theatre changes a lot of what you have decided to do in rehearsal. With this move can come a great sense of loss and of feeling as though you were being thrust into a new environment in front of a vast sea of empty chairs.

Blocking Adjustments

There are some strategies to use when making the adjustment from rehearsal room to the stage space. Remember that the director will be seeing the action from a distance for the first time and will probably need to make a number of blocking adjustments. You must be open to these changes as they happen. It will be slow going at first, so try to be patient; everyone, including the director, will eventually find his/her bearings. Try to mark all of your entrances and exits first. The space may either seem smaller or larger depending on where you have been rehearsing. Pay close attention to how the director is adjusting the other actors from scene to scene. Go over any difficult blocking bits or adjustments at a slow pace to get used to the changes. It may be wise to watch others from the audience to give you a sense of how the set works and where the sight lines are located. By watching other actors, you may be able to tell where you need to make an adjustment in your own work. As the director makes changes, don't fight them; remember he is there as your third eye.

Vocal Adjustments

Acoustics vary from theatre to theatre, and you will need to test out your voice in the space to determine how easy or difficult it is for you to be heard and understood. Do a quick warm-up in the theatre, and try to determine how your voice sounds. Some theatres are kinder to the lower register voices (alto, baritone, or bass sounds); some, to the higher (tenor or soprano sounds). Try to locate all the dead spots in the audience and on stage; it is unfortunate but every theatre has them. Have another cast member listen to you from different seats in the house. Choose some of your quiet moments and a few of your more forceful ones for comparison. The audience should never need to strain to hear you. If you have been working in a more intimate space, you may have become used to reaching the director who was only three feet away. You now have an entire audience to play for and you need to be heard clear to the back row. Some actors overcompensate when they enter a larger space and push their volume before finding out what level is actually needed. You don't want the audience to feel as though you are overprojecting, so choose the appropriate volume for the appropriate moment.

Technical Rehearsals

All the adjustments you will need to make in this transfer from re-hearsal to stage space can lead to some very positive changes in your performance. It is essential to get used to the theatre before the technical and dress rehearsals begin. Use your time in the space efficiently. Keep in mind that once lights, sound, costumes, make-up, and the finishing touches on the set are added, your life will become even more complicated.

The technical and design staff have been working with the director since before rehearsals began in order to establish the environment or "world of the play." When the actors are rehearsing, the shops are building. Hopefully everyone has been working with the same end result in mind. There is a great deal that needs to be coordinated and now is the time to put it all together. In the first technical rehearsals, more than likely, you will be asked to work from cue to cue. There will be a great deal of starting, stopping, and waiting, as the director, designers, and technical crews work through the show to make everything flow smoothly. This is a time to be patient and relaxed. A full-blown performance will be impossible and unnecessary, but you will be expected to be attentive and ready to deliver your lines and complete blocking with timing and accuracy.

Finding Your Light

You will make the lighting designer extremely happy if you can find the "hot" spot wherever you are playing a scene. This is the place where the light has been focused with the most intensity. Looking down on the floor will give you the general area as to where the light is focused. But this can be rather deceiving. You should also look up to see where the hot spot is focused and try to feel it on your face. Audiences can become very frustrated with actors who keep walking into the dark areas of the stage when they are speaking. The light will always be in the general vicinity of where you have been blocked, but you will more than likely have to adjust your position on the stage to find the most intense spot. Some actors are naturals at this, but for others it takes a bit of practice. Also, discover how light functions in the scene and in the production. Come out into the house and watch some of the light cues and scene shifts. By knowing how light is used, you can enhance your performance immeasurably. If you understand the effect, it can only help to give your performance more dimension. If the production is using follow spots, make sure that you hit your mark in the same place every time so the operators can pick you up with ease.

Sound Cues

Sound is one of the more difficult elements to incorporate into any production. Many directors have original scores composed for their shows. Others work with a sound designer to research and find the perfect piece of underscoring or sound effect to highlight the action and your performance. Music and sound effects are there to establish mood, time, place, and even era. Stage actors are much more fortunate than are film actors, as they have the advantage of hearing the music or sound before they give the opening performance. Music can be an invaluable source of inspiration for the actor. Listen to the music and background effects carefully. Work with the music rather than against it.

- Are there any hints in the choice of music or sound that can help you to strengthen a moment?
- What does the music say to you?
- How does it make you feel?
- What is the instrumentation? Are there vocals?
- What is its exact length?

You may need to adjust your volume to be heard over a piece of underscoring. Timing will also be crucial. Music is often strategically placed at a specific moment in the scene. Some directors like to use music to accent the end of a scene and create a smooth transition into the next one. You will need to get used to when music cues begin and end. If you come in too early, your line may be lost; if you are too late, there will be dead time in the action.

As for sound effects, no actor likes to pick up a phone before it has rung, or open the door before someone has knocked. Pay close attention. You will be going back many times to get the sound cues right, and then they will have to be coordinated with the lights and scene shifts. Be patient; the end result is usually very exciting. Whatever you do, do not ignore the sound cues. They can add a great deal to the overall effect of your performance.

Microphones

If you are working in a large space or performing in a musical, there are likely to be microphones placed in specific areas of the stage to enhance your voice or to balance the singing over the orchestra. The use of body microphones is common practice in today's musical theatre. Learn to work with whatever sound enhancement is being used. Give your vocal performance all the energy and intensity you had in rehearsal. Be careful not to get vocally lazy and rely on the microphones to do your work for you. If area microphones are being used, it is a similar experience to finding your light. Find out where the microphones have been hung or placed on the stage. You may need to adjust your position to get the best results. Always work on clear and energized speaking or singing. If you are on a body microphone don't overarticulate ('p's have a tendency to pop and elongated 's's can sound like a whistle). Drive the energy through the final consonants, but don't overdo it. Also make sure you know when your microphone is *hot* (on) when you are backstage. It can be very embarrassing to let the audience in on what is happening when you are out of their view.

Set and Props

In working on the set and with props, remember that safety is paramount. Unless you pay attention to how a set works or a prop functions, you run the risk of getting injured. Some sets are more complicated and confusing than are others, but no matter what the setting, you must always stay sharp and alert. Be aware of the space that you inhabit. With a complicated design, you need to make sure you stay out of everyone's way and follow directions, carefully and quietly, during every scene shift.

There are usually two prop tables set up backstage: one stage left and one stage right. These tables are commonly covered in brown paper and have a clearly marked "home" for each of your props. Treat your props with care. If you use an item, be sure it is returned to its proper place. If you need it preset in a certain place, politely tell someone in charge where it needs to go. Understand how your prop functions. If you break it, make sure you tell someone right away. Remember that nobody is perfect. Check your props before every rehearsal and performance to see they are in the right place and in good working order. You are ultimately responsible for the props you use in the show. It would be extremely embarrassing to walk out on stage only to find an important prop missing or to have it fall apart in your hands. Also, remember to stay off the furniture back stage. There should be chairs set up for the actors; the stage furniture is for use on the stage.

Timing

Timing will be crucial during technical rehearsals. Pay attention to how a cue or series of cues work. Every series of cues has its own rhythm, and the stage manager is often figuring out how to call five cues at the same time. Many cues are taken off an actor, and the timing can get thrown if you are inconsistent. Some actors do not pay enough attention during technical rehearsals and wind up wasting everyone's time when they start to run through the show. If you have a line timed to a technical cue, make sure you are accurate with the words and are speaking it loudly and clearly.

Dress Rehearsals

The final technical elements to be added to the production are the costumes, make-up, wigs, and hairpieces. If you paid attention during your fitting sessions, you should be ready to wear all your costumes. Remember to not let the costume get the better of you. Many period plays will be reproduced with historical accuracy. You will need to look comfortable and natural in what you are wearing rather than looking like an actor wearing or "warring" with a costume. Take great care of what you wear. Hang up your costume after every rehearsal and performance, and make sure all the pieces are there before you leave the dressing room. If you don't like how something fits, then politely explain the problem to the designer or director. Do not complain. Talk through all your concerns with an even temper. If you are allergic to a fabric, let someone know before the costume is built. If it is too tight or too loose, tell them during your fitting. If you find that you just can't do a bit of business the way the costume is constructed, then a compromise is eminent. This may mean that either you get a different costume or you change the blocking. Both options are a possible solution; don't be stubborn and have it be your way or no way at all. Safety is also a consideration. If you have to make an entrance down a stairway wearing a long train or cloak, you don't want to trip and fall. Know how the costume works and remember that practice makes perfect. If you are involved in a quick change, then take the time to practice with your dresser. Always be patient and cooperative.

Some Final Thoughts

All the design elements are there to support your work as an actor. Technical and dress rehearsals can be very fun and are often the most exciting part of putting together a live performance. Remember that many people, especially in an academic or community theatre setting, will be performing their jobs for the first time. Even professional crews need time to get to know how a show works. Be patient. Try not to worry about things that do not concern you. Know your place and adhere to the proper protocol. Go through the proper channels if something isn't working for you. There may have been changes in the design since you were first introduced to it, so always be flexible and ready to adapt to new circumstances. Try not to show your disappointment if something does not work or look the way you expected it to. Above all, thank everyone involved in the production for their hard work and care in making you look your absolute best.

Additional Thoughts for the Director

You are the captain of the ship, the leader of the pack, the conductor of the orchestra and, as such, you will be under a great deal of pressure to make everything work. The actors will be looking to you for inspiration and guidance. Make sure you keep everyone informed at all times. The actors will not know how things work, and so a particularly difficult piece of business will have to be explained before you attempt it for the first time. If it does not work, take the time to go back and fix it. Be sure everyone is comfortable with one moment before you move on to the next. Above all else, let everyone do their job, rather than trying to micromanage. If the actors sense you are tense, they will become so as well. If there is a serious problem, then it needs to be addressed in private and not in public. Bottom line: try to remain calm and friendly at all times.

Performance Notes

Generally speaking, once a show has opened, it is a tradition in the professional theatre that notes from the director are delivered to the actors or posted on the callboard by the stage manager of the production. Protocol in academic and community theatres may vary. The stage manager is ultimately responsible for the run of the show. Her duties include maintaining the integrity of the direction of the play, making sure the show runs smoothly every performance, dealing with any changes the director or actors may want to make, and creating an environment conducive to positive actor morale. Stage managers also give notes about a specific technical requirement that the actor has failed to do correctly, such as a missed line or piece of blocking or an actor who is out of the light. Acting notes should come directly from the director. An actor should never give a note to another actor. If there is a problem with a scene or a moment, the actor should discuss it with the stage manager, who in turn will have a talk with the director or the other actor. Giving another actor a note can cause tremendous problems backstage and in the dressing room.

Some General Notes for the Director

Here are some general guidelines to follow when giving notes to actors in performance. Except for incidental notes such as a blocking adjustment, try not to give too many notes directly after a show. The actors have had a long night and need some downtime after performing. You also may not have the actor's full attention. Light conversation between actor and director is best. Save any complex notes for the next day or post them on the callboard. Take some time to consult with the stage manager after each performance; ask about the general run of the show, the morale of the cast, and the reaction of the audience. Try not to bombard the actors with a series of changes all at once. If you have an inordinate amount of notes for one actor, prioritize them. Allow the actor to make the changes gradually, rather than trying to fix everything at once. If the actors want to make a change, they should discuss it with the stage manager, who will then contact you directly. If you agree with the proposed change, have the stage manager call the actors in early to rehearse the change.

Some General Notes for the Actor

Warming Up

Performing can be a physically, mentally, and emotionally demanding job, requiring a great deal of focused energy. The average length of a play is a little over two hours, but stage time is not real time. Stage time is compressed; what may take only two hours for the actor to perform can be a lifetime for the character. Consequently, the actor needs to be ready to take on the journey of the character every performance.

The best way to be ready to perform is to allow yourself the necessary time to do a complete physical (stretching and aerobic), vocal (projection and diction), and mental (focus and concentration) warm-up before the show. Different warm-ups work for different actors. Here are a few suggestions:

- Try tailoring your warm-up either to the specific play you are in or to the character you are performing.
- As you stretch out, try listening to music that invokes the mood of the play.
- Perform the aerobic part of your warm-up in the manner of your character.
- Speed-through or sing your lines.
- Include special warm-ups such as running difficult fight choreography, lifts, or tricky dance moves.

Musicals will also require you to warm up your singing voice, but remember to attend to your speaking voice as well. Give yourself enough time to ready yourself for performance.

Actors are also athletes, so staying in shape needs to become part of your daily routine. Eat healthfully, drink plenty of water to stay hydrated, consume alcohol in moderation, work out, and remain physically active.

Feeding Your Creativity

The creative process does not stop once the play has opened; there is always room for growth. How often have you closed a show only to realize a week later that you finally understood a specific moment in the play? You wish now you could go back and fix or change your performance, but it is too late. Often those moments come to you at the oddest times, when you are having a conversation with a family member, watching a movie or television show, reading a book, or just walking in the park. The point is that your work is never over. The world is a grand and beautiful adventure. Actors have an obligation to their craft to remain curious about the world they inhabit. The most successful actors are thinking actors, actors who remain hungry about learning, developing their analytical skills, honing their craft, and growing as individuals. Here is a list of things that can help you to grow as an artist and add depth to your process:

- Visit an art museum, art gallery, natural history museum, science museum, zoo, or aquarium.
- Listen to music; go to a concert or music festival.
- Learn how to play a musical instrument.
- Join a choir.
- Learn how to play a new sport.
- Go for a hike or bike ride.
- Go out dancing.
- Spend time in conversation.
- Investigate another culture.
- Watch the news or read the paper daily.
- Read a foreign newspaper or magazine.
- Go to a lecture.
- Go to the movies.
- Visit a library or bookstore.
- Visit a nursing home.
- Try a new restaurant; cook an exotic food.
- Meet new people.
- Read a new play; read an old play.
- Work on a new monologue.
- Take an acting class or a voice lesson.
- Learn a new skill such as juggling, fencing, or horseback riding.

- Read a great philosopher, a biography, or an autobiography.
- Research a period in history you know nothing about.
- Go to a fashion show.
- Travel whenever possible.

As an actor you must remain curious about the world around you and eager to learn of its great riches and fascinating people.

Going Up on a Line

The actor's nightmare is forgetting where you are in the play and consequently going "up" on a line. We have all had momentary lapses of memory in real life, but forgetting a line in front of an audience can be a devastating experience. Your heart races, you start to perspire, and you look with panic in your eyes to your acting partner for help. You have never felt so alone or vulnerable in your life.

First, don't let the audience know that, for the moment, you are lost and panicking. Stay in character. Take a moment to breathe and relax and allow your character the time to think. Hopefully your scene partner will come through for you. If your partner is unsure as well or can't figure a way to cover your line (or if you happen to be on stage alone), remember the audience doesn't know the lines either. Unless you tell them you are lost by projecting this through your behavior, they will never know anything is wrong.

Second, trust yourself. Though you may be unsure about the exact wording of the text, you can at least rely on the fact that you know the story, you know what comes next. So, start to paraphrase until you get back on track. If you can't think of anything to say, go to the first thing you can remember. You can always fix any missed or crucial information later on in the play.

When the shoe is on the other foot and your acting partner goes up on a line, remember she may need help getting out of it. Either ask her a question in character or skip to your next line. Sometimes you may be able to say her line by rephrasing it in your own character's voice. The bottom line is, whether it is you or your partner who is lost in the scene, when you stay relaxed, you find a way out of the predicament.

Staying in Character

Dropping your character in the middle of a scene is extremely confusing to an audience. Different situations can trigger a drop in character. Some incident may happen out of the blue and thus be out of your control: something on the set falls over and startles you, you trip on the set or accidentally bump into another actor, or you lose your balance and fall down. Perhaps your costume gets caught on something, a zipper gets stuck, or you come up short tying your tie. Vocally, you may stumble on your words or stumble on the punch line to a joke. Something may get stuck in your throat or you have to cough or sneeze. Whatever happens, whether it is beyond your control or not, remember to deal with it in character. For instance, how would your character react if they sneezed at an improper moment? How would your character react to tripping over a shoelace? The more human you can make your character, the more believable you will be to an audience.

Some emotional situations may also cause you to lose your character. Perhaps something amuses you as the actor and you want to laugh, or another actor surprises you with unrehearsed changes that make you angry. Maybe your timing is off; you either are having a bad night and can't get back on track or are not getting the kind of response from the audience you anticipated. Whether consciously or not, your response to these situations becomes manifested physically, and the audience can pick up on your body language. Whatever the situation, try not to show your "actor" emotions when on stage. Concentrate on the action of the scene. Pay special attention to the moments when you are not the focal point of the action; often this is when you are least aware that you have dropped the mask of the character. Remember that you need to be physically engaged in the action at all times. Whatever the situation or circumstance, you have an obligation to both the audience and your fellow actors to stay in character.

Keeping It Fresh

Once the play has opened and the actors begin to settle into a long run, there is always the danger of either becoming bored with your role or taking the action of the play for granted. To keep the performance fresh demands an inordinate amount of concentration and commitment from the actors. Some actors even begin to add new bits and unrehearsed choices just to relieve the boredom. But performance freedom is not the same as the improvisational freedom so necessary in the rehearsal room. The actor should always rehearse a new idea or line reading with the director, before adding it to the performance. Resist your impulse to change something out of sheer boredom. Directors who see the play after it has been running for awhile often have to take out the "improvements" the actors have made and get them back on course with what was rehearsed.

Just as the characters in a play, we live our lives from moment to moment. In the theatre, every performance is slightly different. Remember the audience is seeing and hearing the play for the first time.

Using good listening technique, pay attention to what the other actors are giving you. Keep one ear focused on the action of the scene and one on the audience reaction.

Another valuable technique is to offer up your performance to someone very close to you, such as a loved one or someone who is a source of constant inspiration to you. During your warm-up or right before you go on stage, allow yourself a few minutes of meditation on the person to whom you are going to dedicate the show. Then let it go and think about your first entrance. Doing this will help you to invest energy and focus into your performance.

Allowing for Spontaneity

Spontaneous behavior in life is very different from spontaneously responding within the structured world of a play. When we are spontaneous in life, we adopt a carefree attitude, letting go of our organized everyday life for a bit of unplanned adventure. But when acting, spontaneity is connected to the playing out of an organized and rehearsed set of choices. Spontaneous reactions take many forms. Perhaps you really hear a word for the first time, add a subtle glance where you never did before, or notice a reaction from another actor that changes your response. You may suddenly be struck by a new meaning or a deeper understanding of a line that you thought you understood completely before.

The best way to allow for spontaneity in your performance is to trust your original choices. This will ensure a clear telling of the story and allow spontaneous thoughts to occur. If a spontaneous action does occur, allow it to color the choices you have already made. This will add new dimension to your performance and keep the action of the play alive for you night after night.

Continuing to Grow with the Character

The opening of a show is certainly not the end of your process as an actor. In a way, it is merely the beginning. With the necessary addition of the audience comes the opportunity to fine-tune your portrayal of the character and to make any adjustments that might make your performance richer and more satisfying. Remember that theatre is a living art form. Just like a good wine, the live performance of a play gets better with time.

The opportunity for your work to grow, for your character to achieve subtlety and nuance, is part of the excitement of live performance. Moments may change; you may gain a new insight on a specific line or even a relationship; the audience may teach you something you had not considered before. To paraphrase Stanislavsky, the art of acting is the art of creating a new human and that human comes into existence with each and every performance of the play.

Working with the Audience

Actors love to blame the audience for an "off" night. How often have you heard an actor talking in the dressing room after the show complaining about how terrible the audience was?

"They aren't laughing in the right places."

"They aren't laughing at all."

"They usually cry at that moment, I can always hear the sniffles."

"That applause was lukewarm."

"They seem bored."

"They just don't like me."

Every audience is different and unique. They will never respond in exactly the same place, with the same amount of laughter or applause. Since the advent of television and, specifically, the situation comedy, we as a culture have become used to constant applause and laughs. When an audience is assembled in the studio for the taping of a television show, they are attending for no charge. All they are asked to do is respond with laughter and applause when signaled.

But in the theatre, you are performing for paying customers who have the right to respond in their own manner and at their own whim. Blaming the audience for being unreceptive to the play is counterproductive. A negative attitude will only infringe on your performance. This attitude may even coax you into altering something, which is unfair to your fellow performers and detrimental to the outcome of the play. Learn to work with and embrace the individuality of an audience. Some are quiet and some are more vocal. Just because an audience is quiet does not mean they are not enjoying the performance. They may merely be listening on a deeper level. Whatever the situation, remember the audience is not your enemy; they truly are there to enjoy themselves and you.

Taking Off the Mask in the Curtain Call

The ritual of the curtain call serves several purposes. It is a chance for the audience to recognize and applaud the effort of the actors. It functions as a transition, for both the actors and the audience, from the imaginary circumstances of the play back into the "real world." It is also an opportunity for the actors to face the audience as themselves and to acknowledge the fact that they were only playing roles. This is unique to live theatre because in movies or television we do not have the privilege of thanking the actors in person. The curtain call brings the play to a close, and the audience needs and appreciates having a formal ending to the theatrical event.

Sometimes actors look or feel awkward in the curtain call. Because this is the audience's final impression of you, bows need the same care and attention given to other elements of the performance. Actors who communicate through their attitude that they are uncomfortable taking a bow or that they don't really want to be there, turn the audience off. Receiving a compliment can be difficult for some actors. If you feel awkward accepting applause, remember a bow is a sign of humility. You lower your head to show you are gracious and appreciative of their attention. If you are told that you come across as having an attitude or appear affected, consciously use your bow as a means to thank the audience for the privilege of performing. In this manner, you will be presenting yourself as an actor with a professional demeanor, respectful of and grateful to your paying audience.

Conversely, some actors have trouble breaking away from their characters and facing the audience as themselves. If a role is exhausting or emotional, it can be especially challenging for an actor to drop the character and immediately produce a smile for the audience. But appearing grim or distraught in the curtain call makes the actor seem indulgent or even self-absorbed. While big, radiant smiles may only be appropriate for comedies or musicals, more subtle smiles are quite suitable for serious plays. If you have trouble leaving your character behind, think of the bows as a chance to celebrate the character, the play, and the theatrical experience. It is a moment of release, a chance to take off the mask of the character.

Occasionally, directors will decide to eliminate the curtain call or to have the actors stay in character during the applause. While these techniques may be effective in very specific cases, usually they leave the audience frustrated and confused, needing and wanting to express their appreciation but being thwarted in doing so. It is best to give it a lot of thought before deciding either to abandon a curtain call or to play it in character.

Additional Thoughts for the Director

When watching the play in performance, you need to keep your eyes and ears open to how the audience is responding. Are they restless at certain moments, squirming in chairs, getting up and down, coughing?

Is a laugh line falling flat? Is something on stage distracting them? You should also pay attention to how well the story is being told. Are the plot points clear? Are the beat shifts strongly delineated? Do the transitions from scene to scene run smoothly? Be especially aware of actors who have a tendency to rush when in front of an audience and drop important information along the way. The clarity of the moment can also suffer due to poor diction and projection. Watch for an actor who is "overplaying" a moment, either by going for a cheap laugh or by becoming too emotional. Of course, it is always satisfying when one can move an audience to laughter or tears, but a cheap laugh or cry must not be the actor's primary objective. Watch for consistency in each actor's performance. Are the "important" moments clear and centered? If an actor is either going too far or pulling too far back from a key moment, he loses believability and muddies the action. Make sure key moments are played with a balance of emotion and intellect.

Conversations with Directors

Six professional directors, from across the United States, share some of their approaches to the rehearsal process and their thoughts about giving notes.

Libby Appel

Libby Appel was interviewed in her office at the Oregon Shakespeare Festival.

Can you talk about the relationship you like to establish with actors?

Libby Appel: I would say I have a general approach, which is collaborative. By that I mean I don't go into rehearsals with a set idea, and I don't even cast with a set idea of the character in my mind. I have a very clear idea of what the play is saying and what I want to say with the play, but not the specifics on the character. So I really use a lot of intuition, even in the casting process. I'm not looking for my idea to be fulfilled, but for the whole cast to spark off of one another so we can find stuff that I never could have imagined in the first place. And that's what I think is the collaborative process, for me anyway. I go into this totally selfishly. I go into this to get a thrill out of the discovery process, and that's what happens when people feel safe and feel that they can share together in a way that brings out creative and imaginative solutions to things.

How do you create that sense of safety?

Libby Appel: I know my play well. I've done my homework, and I think actors know that. So there's confidence immediately: "Oh, she knows what she's talking about." I try to express what I believe are the major themes of the play, what I want to emphasize, and where the design decisions came from, so they know the world of the play we're trying to create, and they can fit into that world. And then we sit and read for a few days. After that I begin the staging process, but I do it very much in collaboration with the actors. In other words, I don't stage at home. I know where the entrances and exits are, but I don't stage at home. I do it with them, and we work it out based upon what we already know about the text. It's done with that collaborative spirit of "Why don't you try that?" "No wait. Let me try this." "Oh yeah, that's much better." All of that leads to what I think is an atmosphere in which people feel safe to work. They know that I'm not going to stamp on them and that I'm going to respect what they have to offer. I think that's the key, now that we're just saying it. I think respect is the answer. I respect them, and I hope they respect me. So from there we can work together as artists.

How would you characterize your rehearsal process?

Libby Appel: I want results, but my process isn't about results. I'm very much focused on layering. In other words, I'll do a rough staging with the actors, and then we'll go back in and go at it again. And then we'll go back in and go at it again. Usually four rounds of that before we get a real run-through. And sometimes I'll stage a scene that's just a bloody mess, you don't even want to look it's so horrible. I don't care about that to begin with. I can't stand to look at it, but I know I'll fix it. Often an actor will say, "It's a mess and what do we do?" And I say, "Don't worry about that. I'm great at the end. I'll fix it all at the end. But what's this moment about? We haven't found out what this moment is about yet." And no matter how much homework I do in advance, I don't really understand the scenes until the actors are in there.

How do you watch a run-through? Do you try to clear your mind of what you saw the day before?

Libby Appel: I will ask, "Am I telling the story?" and "What's missing in the story?" I'm not thinking, "Wait a minute! They missed that moment!" I never care about the piece of business that we might have taken two hours to develop. If it's gone, it's gone. If something new happens and it is better, I don't get stuck on what we've developed. Nothing is that precious; it can all be thrown out. The question is are we telling the story in a rich, provocative, and challenging way?

What typical notes do you give?

Libby Appel: I'm always stressing how we can communicate this play, how we're telling this story, and what the shape is. And I want the actors to be part of that process. So I'm always communicating, "We're dropping this plot line here." And sometimes I won't know how to make it better; I'll only say that. "How can we make it better?" And then somebody will say, "You know, I have that line that I can stress a little bit more." And of course they're right. And I hadn't thought of that. I'll share the dilemma of where we're going and what we still have to do, and get some help from them.

I give notes right through previews, even if the show is in very good shape. I bring the actors together after each preview, even if we're not going to rehearse anything, just to give some general notes and a few specifics. And I will always say, "Is there anything you want to work on? Now don't be shy, just because your partner is rolling his eyes. If there's something that's left undone for you, let's work on it." Obviously, if there are things undone for me, we will work tiny moments. I love that; I love doing that during previews. But I'll always work for what the actor wants to do as well.

I think of myself toward the end as an editor. I'm helping an actor clean up his or her performance, as opposed to creating that performance. So my notes are responding to the things I see, and often as I do this, a new idea will come. So the note will be, "You know when you were doing that, suddenly it occurred to me that..." You start to see another possibility because of what that person is doing. Something that person hadn't thought of, nor had I thought of before, but in the chemistry of the moment it comes out.

What advice would you give to new directors regarding giving notes?

Libby Appel: The most important thing is to know your play well. Go back and read your play every night after your rehearsal is over, so you really feel as if this play is inside your body. But don't know it so well that you have an idea of how everything should be said and done. Be willing and open to collaborate. So my suggestion is to keep it about the inquiry, not about being right.

Anne Bogart

Anne Bogart sat for an interview at Columbia University.

What relationship do you like to have with actors?

Anne Bogart: What I look for is the actor who never uses the word "want," as in "Is this what you want?" Because that's a horrible disease. I'd rather make a proposition and they come back with something different. Not necessarily negating what I've done but adding onto it. I'm the initiator and I create the circumstances, the atmosphere in which something can happen. That's my job. And my job is to point a direction. A director does that, point the direction. But once I've done that, the actor has to come back to me with something else. Not the same as what I've said. But something that either adds to or disagrees with it, not in a paralyzing way but in a creative way. I look for actors who are smart, who are talented and who are spontaneous and flexible—who are tenacious, usually more tenacious than I am. I usually give up too early. I need actors who will—and my company does this—they'll stay up all night in a bar while I'm sleeping and they'll come up to me the next day and say, "Well we think the second act belongs after the third act." So I need actors who are active collaborators.

How do you see your role as director?

Anne Bogart: The smartest thing I've ever heard in my whole life was what a Russian actress said: "An actor's job is to direct the role." And I think that's the most profound thing you can say to a director, "Your job is not to direct the role. Your job is to direct the play." If you realize the actor has to direct the role and you set up the circumstances in which the actor is directing the role and you're directing the play, then you're probably going to have a creative relationship. But if you're trying to direct the role and the play, you're going to get in trouble. And an actor has to realize that too; their job is to direct the role, not to wait to be told what to do.

For example, an actor comes on stage and looks at somebody else and says the first line and I'll say, "Well, what do you want the audience to learn about you that they didn't know already?" "I guess that she's in love and she's scared." "I didn't see that." And so they go out again. It comes from them. It's not me saying, "Now enter. Be in love and scared." I don't do that. But I do ask them questions. And then they have to, in the Brechtian sense, show me.

And do you know ahead of time you want the actor to enter and be scared, or are you asking the question waiting for the actor to come up with it?

Anne Bogart: Mostly I'm waiting for the actor to come up with it. I'll tell them everything that I know for sure. I do that before a rehearsal. I have a list of everything I know for sure, and then all the things I don't know. And I'll read them out loud. Hopefully during the table work, which is pretty extensive, I've gotten that all out of my system. I "download it," everything that I've been thinking about for how many years I've been thinking about this play. And they have all that information. And then I just watch them; I'm looking and I'm listening.

How do you know when to give a note, when an actor is ready to listen?

Anne Bogart: That's all intuitive. What you can say is you have to feel it, in the same way as in a love relationship. When do you say, "I love you" for the first time? Do you think about it? Well, that's going to ruin it. You're in the moment and you try to be sensitive to what's the right moment and what's not the right moment. And that comes from reading the situation. Which means go back to listening, listening, be attentive, looking, reading it. Directors think too much that their job is to make things happen; it's actually to listen. To read the situation.

I once couldn't go to a rehearsal of a show and I'd asked a young director to go and sit in for me. He knew the show very well. The next day I asked one of the actors in the company, Ellen Lauren, I said "How did he do?" She said, "Not very well." I said, "Why?" She said, "Well, he didn't say anything. As an actor, I almost don't care what he says, but the fact that he says something allows me to organize myself around that observation. Even if he says 'I noticed your hand on the door at this moment and that was interesting to me.' " Or anything so she could organize herself around an observation. So I think her point is really true. A director needs to not be too egotistical and not worry about whether or not you're saying the right thing. But that you make an attempt at the observation is more important sometimes than the observation be a "correct" one.

What are the typical kinds of notes you give?

Anne Bogart: I give a lot of spatial notes. I have an obsessive need for spatial harmony. So I give a lot of notes about, "Could you do this three inches to the right?" Literally I can't stand it unless there's a harmonic composition on the stage. I know there's a certain balance that I crave. And the actors I work with really get it; they understand the aesthetics of my obsessive compositional sense.

I concentrate a lot on space, not because I think that's ultimately what we are doing, but in a way, the real work I have to stay out of the way of. What the actor is *really* doing, I have no business getting in there. I don't deal with psychology very much after the table work. I deal with issues of where your hand is or where your foot is. I don't believe in this misunderstanding of the Stanislavski system, which was done by Mr. Strasberg where you get inside the actor's emotions; I don't believe in setting the emotions. So a lot of my attention is on things I'm actually not as interested in. I'm, of course, interested in emotionality, and passion and clarity and articulation, but you don't go at that by saying, "Okay, be really emotional." You go at it by saying, "Try putting your hand a little further to the right at this moment." And oddly enough, if you were watching my rehearsal you'd say, "God, she's really interested in superficial things." But in fact that's not what I'm interested in. You can't look directly at the sun, because it would burn your eyes. You have to look to the side, but you're actually interested in the sun. And that's what I'm doing in rehearsal. I'm looking to the side at issues of time and space, but I'm actually interested in the human experience. But I don't think you can go right there. You just hope that it comes along.

You've written about the moment when you know something is not working on stage and you have to leave your place and walk toward the stage without an idea, and during that walk you find an idea.

Anne Bogart: I was talking to my friend Molly Smith who is artistic director of the Arena Stage; she's a really great old friend. She used to run the Perseverance Theatre in Alaska. She's very Alaskan. And I said, "Molly, you're about the best leader I know." And she said, "Let me tell you something. This is what I think about. A kayaker in Alaska knows that if you're in a river, and you suddenly come fast upon a rock, the tendency is to want to lean away from it to get the kayak away from this rock. Actually, it's counterintuitive, but the way you have to deal with the situation, and kayakers learn this, you actually have to lean into the rock. And that's the only way you'll get away from the rock." And I think that's the thing. In rehearsal it's not about thinking it out first and then acting on it. You lean before you know what you are going to say. You actually have to physically move in the direction where there's a conflict or problem and then something's got to happen. It's leaning into the rock.

Scott Ellis

Scott Ellis took a few minutes during the break of technical rehearsals of a Broadway musical.

What do you see as your job as director?

Scott Ellis: The thing I always think about directing is that it's like a tightrope. The actors are on this tightrope. They're going to fall sometimes. You've got to make sure there's a net to catch them so they don't get hurt, because then they'll climb back up and try it again. Pretty soon they'll get across that tightrope, and then they're going to cross it again and they'll be really good at it. But at the beginning they have to know there's a net, because it's frightening to go and explore a character. When they know it's there, they're okay falling on their face or trying something that doesn't work. They'll get back up and try it again. But if they feel they don't have that safety net, they get really scared, and they clench up and fall and hurt themselves.

How do you create that net?

Scott Ellis: First of all I take a long time with casting, and I try to put together people who I know I want to work with for six weeks. I think one of my strongest points is casting. I've learned to have a fairly good eye with it, and it takes me a long time to do it.

I try to have a relaxed environment. I like laughing. I like being sarcastic. I like just being a little looser so people feel free to be so as well. I would say when you come into a room an actor's wall is half up, and you can slowly, slowly, by trust, get that wall to drop down. But if you don't, that wall creeps up and, once it's up, it will never drop again. Because they're putting themselves on the line, there's always going to be that feeling that they should be protected. So you always have this wall of "Can I trust you? Is it okay?" And if you can give them that feeling of trust, then the wall drops and there's a real working relationship.

Actors pick up the energy and mood of the director. How do you stay calm amidst all the chaos?

Scott Ellis: You know, I've gotten better. In fact, recently a stage manager came up and thanked me for not throwing any tantrums, which I don't do, though I know some directors do. I always try to keep it as calm as I can, because basically the director is the captain of the ship, and if I start freaking, everyone will start freaking. In difficult situations, I'm always in the back of my mind thinking about where I'm heading. I put goals up there, what I want to get through. And that seems to help. It sets the tone. And if it's a tense situation, everyone is tense. It just happens. Just try to keep relaxed.

Some of the actors we have interviewed have talked about a director's ability to know when to give a note and when to hold off on a note.

Scott Ellis: It's very important, very important, because your mind as a director is constantly moving. You're thinking, "That doesn't work; okay, this is what we need to do next." But if you give the actors too much you won't get anything back, so you have to really select when the moment is right. I think it's an instinct because every actor is different; every actor is on his own journey, his own sort of track. So you're constantly thinking, "This guy has got to point A, but the other guy has got to get to point E," so you have to have different notes to guide them with. And some actors want more notes, and others you have to pull back a little bit, so it's a constant juggling to feel out what's needed.

One thing I always have to work on is giving positive notes, which I tend not to do. I'm always after the things that I know can be better, and I usually have to tell actors that up front. I'm not the type, this is just me personally, that says, "Oh that was just perfect! Great." I usually don't. I usually say, "If I don't say anything it means I'm happy with it." Which is okay. But sometimes you have to balance it.

What kinds of notes do you give?

Scott Ellis: An actor can see the journey of the character, but he has to have a third eye to help him shape that journey, the arc. If a character moves from point A to point M, there's a lot of places in between that he's going to be going, and sometimes an actor doesn't see that. You have to really look at it and get very specific about the events, when there's an intention change, where the obstacles are, and orchestrate them in a way. And the journey constantly changes, because once you get it to one point, something else happens and then it moves to another place, so it's constantly changing. And you shape it hand-in-hand with an actor.

What do you do when an actor disagrees with a note?

Scott Ellis: You try to talk it through. You try to see their point of view. You try to get them to see your point of view. Ultimately, I can't make actors do anything they are uncomfortable with because it's not going to work. It's just not going to work. So I've got to find us some way to get around it. If they just don't understand an idea, or they're confused by it, I've got to find different tacks. I'll never say my way is the only way because then you're hitting horns and there's no reason to do that. Maybe there is a better way. If it's not working, and it's clear it's not working, you both have to say "This isn't working; I think we need to find a better way to do this." So you try to have respect for them.

But I can become very passionate if I really feel it's warranted. I'll never forget, I was working with this very talented actor and I was extremely scared. We had this scene which was really hard and it was not working, but I had a very strong feeling about how it went. I kept pushing him to do something that I thought was really right. And I kept gently pushing and making him do the scene again and finally it clicked! One time it clicked. And he knew it clicked, and I knew it clicked. So sometimes you do that, you keep trying.

In long runs, do you come back and give notes?

Scott Ellis: Oh sure. I "take out" notes. Some shows stay much better, other shows loosen up a little bit. But sometimes actors just forget, and the stakes aren't very high anymore. They get used to the laughs and can let the audience guide them, which can be very dangerous. So you just have to get them back on track and remind them what was the core of what they were doing.

Any last advice?

Scott Ellis: I have to remind myself that you always have to start at the beginning and ask questions all over again. Sometimes you think, "Oh, I can just jump ahead." But no, you can't jump ahead: you just can't. That's probably the hardest thing, just going back to the basics. It's always going back to the basics. For a long time now when I start rehearsals, I read Uta Hagen's book, *Respect* *for Acting,* because it centers me. It gives me a base to begin the work all over again. A *new* journey.

D. Scott Glasser

D. Scott Glasser was interviewed in a coffee shop near his office at the Madison Repertory Theatre.

Talk about how you like to take notes.

D. Scott Glasser: Frankly, I don't want to ever take my attention away from the actors. I have a good memory for notes. When I have the script in front of me, which continues right up until we're in the theatre, I put some kind of inscrutable marks in the margin for each note: perhaps an "X," an infinity symbol, a red circle. Something fast and efficient. All it does is mark the place in the script where I want to give a note. Sometimes I write a one-word description, for example, "pace" or "re-stage" or "clarify." A question mark usually means "I don't understand what you're talking about" or "I can't hear you." The only photographic memory I have is for what transpired during that previous performance, run-through, or rehearsal. My goal is to be glued to what's happening among the actors in rehearsal, with no distractions. I don't even glance away. I can't imagine reading a newspaper and saying "Let me know what you come up with." I'm sitting in the middle of the action, that's what it feels like. Every moment is imprinted on my memory. And I'm breathing with the actors. I can sense when they're lost. I know when the bottom drops out of the scene. It's clear where we haven't attended to the play with clarity. Then I can serve the actors' needs. If actors believe you're working with them, they really do want to know, "How did this moment work? I tried this, was it okay?" If I'm not wholly there with them how can I respond?

What kind of general notes do you give?

D. Scott Glasser: When I give notes to the full cast, I try to give perspective as to where we are in the process. So, I'm always trying to say, "This is where we are. Where we are is fine." And I truly believe that if we are working together aggressively, wherever we are truly is fine. And we move forward from here. After all, theatre is a constantly shifting organism. Though one has a vision of where the work is headed, and you do your damnedest to enable it to get there, there can be no finite state. Though you are always aiming for perfection, it cannot be achieved. So, notes state where we are, what seems to be working or not, and how we move forward from here. The work evolves from first rehearsal to final performance.

How do you watch a rehearsal?

D. Scott Glasser: I like to stand in the rehearsal hall, with my script on a music stand. I don't like sitting; I want to have my energy up. If I sit I become a passive observer. I want to be an active observer. I want to have the same energy the actors have. I move around the rehearsal hall or theatre to make certain we are telling the story to audiences on all sides and at all distances. I tend to avoid dead center, even in the rehearsal hall.

You've worked with professional actors and nonprofessionals in the same production. Do your notes shift?

D. Scott Glasser: With the goal of having the entire ensemble performing from the same understanding of the play and production, I use the rehearsal time according to the needs of each cast. Sometimes this necessitates spending more time with those who haven't reached a certain level than with those who have. I might not give as much attention to an actor who understands the concept and the process and is confidently moving forward than to one who is stumbling. This can be frustrating for accomplished actors. After all, most actors don't just want to be good; they want to be brilliant. And they expect help to get there. Still, if someone in a key role is lost, I need to attend to them.

What do you do when an actor gets worse after a note?

D. Scott Glasser: I say, "I made a big, big mistake. Boy, was I wrong. It was of great value to explore that, and what we just learned is that is not the way to approach that moment. Now let's try something else."

Have you had an actor make a suggestion that was out in left field? How did you handle the situation?

D. Scott Glasser: Yes. Without laughing or making the actor feel stupid, I indicated that it was an interesting point of view, but that it is really a red herring. It would lead in a direction that is a dead end in the play. I made clear the reasons why, and that I could see why he would be led to that idea, but I firmly said that I did not think he should go there. He thought about it and came back to me and said, "I hear what you're saying and it makes sense and I'm going to rethink my approach." So, the actor never felt he had been humiliated.

How about when friends give notes to cast members?

D. Scott Glasser: That can be disastrous. It's often counter to the needs of the show. If they weren't in the rehearsal process, their ideas could be from another agenda about the actor or character. It can destroy confidence and prevent an actor from taking risks. It can be insidious.

Joseph Hanreddy

Joseph Hanreddy met for an interview at his office at the Milwaukee Repertory Theatre.

What is your approach to giving notes during run-throughs?

Joseph Hanreddy: You really want to give a hell of a lot more praise notes than cautionary notes; make it a three-to-one ratio. Or you don't give notes. You will have run-throughs where it really felt hard. Somebody's concentration was bad; we really weren't ready to do a run; somebody had a headache; somebody's girlfriend left him this morning. You have a lot of rehearsals to screw up so don't give a lot of notes on it. It just means you have to work it one more time before you run it. Instead, you go through the moments and reinforce the positive. But it does not do anybody a lot of good if you have a really bad run-through, to have you talk about how bad it was for three hours. It's not as though somebody walked away thinking it was good. I have rarely had that, where somebody was under the misdirected illusion that this was really, really good. Usually they walk away from it saying, "I really just need another crack at it." And sometimes, if you don't have the time to run it again, just let everybody go early, get some rest, and come back and do it again. Again, the negative reinforcement is not going to make it better in my experience

I try to the best of my ability to never give a note that starts with "don't." In other words, "don't sit here," or "I don't like it when you do that." "Don't look at the floor." "Don't scratch your nose." Certainly you have watched a run-through when your first reaction is "don't do that." But keep your eye out from the actor's standpoint and try to find something that you can say: "go towards this there," "go forward; don't go backward," because then the next time actors come to that moment, all they've got is a negative reinforcement for something they did the last time. It takes them out of that moment each time. Whereas, if you phrase it in terms of the fundamentals of action—I really believe in that—you give the actor a task to keep them going forward.

Do you give notes right away?

Joseph Hanreddy: Yes, I try to. The overnight process for the actor is pretty important. What works best for me is to give the notes right after the run-through. The actors write them down in their journals, they wake up the next morning, they look at the notes, remember how they are going to get that in the show, and they do it. The big thing is to try to avoid having the actors think about the notes while they are doing the next run-through.

What do you see as your job as a director?

Joseph Hanreddy: One idea that helps, and this is not my analogy, is to think of the director's job essentially as determining the direction of the voyage that's going to be taken. We are going to leave New York on an ocean liner and here is where we are going. However, the ideal is that everybody will be involved in the process of determining the route, including the actors.

If an actor is ideally cast, and they are a great actor, anybody can direct them. You are only as good as how well you can help an actor in trouble. If you have a great actor, and I have been really blessed with some powerhouse talents in my shows, then you just want to make sure you have enough of a connection with that person so they're confident to use you as a tool to help refine their work. Sometimes you are there merely to make sure that the runway is clear for them to do what they need to do. As a director, you don't need to prove your need or value to the production. If somebody comes in ready to play a role and they are already great at it, they may have a hell of a lot more to teach you than you have to give them. Part of your concentration is on what is going on around them, how the mise-en-scène is going to best help them be what they need to be. Certainly you also try to connect with them and let them know you are available and there for them. You send little messages to let them know you are listening. If all of their choices are good, sometimes you just need to articulate them, "I got this out of what you did, etc." But, don't give a note just to prove you are there. And at the same time, if somebody is floundering, then you need to go back to the fundamentals. If the actor has casting doubts, "I don't see myself in this role," then sometimes the discussion is about, "What part of yourself can we use to get you there?"

I think we have all made mistakes as directors. "That was the last thing that actor needed to hear, I thought that was going to be so helpful, and now I've put them back another week. Now I have to undo something that I said; I drew attention to something that was the last thing they wanted to look at." You have to be careful.

Does how you communicate to actors change from play to play?

Joseph Hanreddy: I think it is important to set the tone that this is not just another play. This is a play that requires us as a group to put ourselves in the same environment. Whether the environment is harsh or whether it's witty and urbane—it has to be embraced by the entire group. It can't be, "Oh, we'll just have fun doing this." If the environment of the play is rough and abrasive, sometimes it requires a little bit of "edgy" energy in the way we communicate to each other. It doesn't mean that you are actually pretending to be somebody else, but you are certainly trying to maintain a certain ambiance in the hall so the energy or tone doesn't really drop out or go away, except during the breaks. I do find that my own physical energy, communicative energy, choice of words, choice of voice tone take on a little bit of that emotional tone, just so everybody stays in there, so that it doesn't become intellectual.

Bill Rauch

Bill Rauch was interviewed in a downtown Los Angeles restaurant, near the Cornerstone Theater offices.

What relationship do you like to have with your actors?

Bill Rauch: I think the relationship I have with actors is as a collaborator first and foremost, and as a cheerleader—I think I'm a big cheerleader in terms of affirming choices. Even when I don't feel a choice an actor made is what I wanted, I want to affirm the fact that he went out on a limb in the first place. So I think I do a lot of cheerleading.

Describe your rehearsal process and how note giving fits into it.

Bill Rauch: I try to work on small beats, as small as possible, early on in a rehearsal. We start by reading and talking through everything, but then, as we get into digging into a scene, I start working in very small beats. When I observe directors that are inexperienced, the first issue I have is that they always run and run and run, and they don't break it down and really work on the small increments. I really only start taking notes when we go into run-through mode.

How do you address the full company when you have a general meeting? Is there a mood you try to set?

Bill Rauch: I try to talk about how far I think we've come, and what we need to still shoot for. I try to hit on a theme of the rehearsal we've just had or the rehearsal we're about to have. For example, "The last few days have been about getting everything technically right, so tonight is really about finding the spirit of the show again." Or, "Tonight I want everything to be sloppy but really committed emotionally. And if things are sloppy, that's okay, because it's important to bite into the emotional life." Or, "Tonight it's time to pull everything back down a notch, let everything become more subtle, and a lot simpler." Whatever I feel is what the show needs.

How about when you give a note and you see the actor really trying hard and tensing up at that moment?

Bill Rauch: I am a voracious note taker—voracious is the proper word—and I give lots of notes. I give notes during the performance runs, but I have learned that when I miss a show, it has a special energy because nobody is focused on trying to remember my notes. So many times when lines get dropped or things get messed up, it's because the actor is concentrating on trying to nail the note rather than on flying with impulses. And so I've really learned the value of not giving notes.

What do you do when an actor isn't taking a note?

Bill Rauch: The thing I'm learning as I get older is to trust my own stomach. In other words, if I'm getting really tense about why an actor won't take a note, instead of immediately thinking "I can't believe that actor is not taking that note!," I recognize there's a real problem and I come at it from a different angle. "I've said this note a couple of times and obviously it isn't working. Can you tell me what to do to help?" It's empowering the actor to find a way for me to communicate something more effectively. One of the things I say more often now is "There's something about this moment that's not working. I don't know what it is. How do you feel? Do you feel the moment is working? Do you have any ideas about what we might try in this moment?" And just being really honest. And it's hard, I think as directors we're afraid of looking not in control or looking like we don't know what we're doing. But I actually think if you really come at it from your heart and are honest with an actor, you can go much farther and much deeper.

How do you know an actor is open to hear what you have to say?

Bill Rauch: It's very interesting. You may do damage if you keep harping at a note again and again. There comes a point if an actor doesn't take a note you've given four or five times, the problem may not be with the actor, the problem may well be with your note. And it may be that you're locked into a tunnel vision about how the moment should be played, instead of trying to find a way the moment will work for that actor. Or you're not communicating the note effectively; you need to find a different way of communicating your notes.

Do you ever find that actors worry about other actors?

Bill Rauch: Actors giving notes to other actors—that's a biggie, especially with inexperienced actors. I find that they can often pipe up and start saying how they think another actor should be in a scene. And those are very sensitive moments. I think it's really exciting that they have an impulse to think about the big picture, and that's an impulse that should be honored. It's great, but obviously actors don't like getting notes from other actors, and they shouldn't.

What do you say?

Bill Rauch: I say, "It's wonderful that you're thinking about the whole scene, but it's best to keep your ideas coming through me instead of turning and giving them to the other actor, because it's confusing for actors to get notes from lots of different people." Sometimes I say this privately, but sometimes it's important to do it publicly, because the other actors are freaked out and they need to see I'm dealing with the situation right in that moment. The other thing to say is, "That's great that you're thinking about their character, but now try to think about that problem from the perspective of your character. How can *your* character make that happen on stage?"

If you were to give advice to a director starting out what would it be?

Bill Rauch: Be sensitive about communicating your impatience to an actor. I think directors rolling their eyes when an actor does something wrong is so damaging to an actor. And I think it goes back to putting yourself in the actor's shoes and how you would want to be treated. You don't have to be disrespectful in order to assert your authority, and ultimately you end up a lot less authoritative if you're disrespectful.

The beautiful thing about art is that there is no right. There are a million right ways a moment can be played, and there are a million things that can go wrong with a moment. And so you just have to find one right that happens to work for you and that actor in that room in that moment in time. And you get to just pick one of the dozens of those rights that may come to you as collaborators.

Conversations with Actors

Five Broadway actors reflect on their experiences with collaboration in rehearsal.

André De Shields

André De Shields took time after a matinee of *The Full Monty* for an interview.

What is the ideal director/actor relationship in your view?

André De Shields: I've been in this industry professionally for thirty-one years, not only as an actor but also as a director and a teacher. And what I'm discovering still, is that collaboration is most effective when the director says "jump" and the actor says "how high?" End of story. Not end of collaboration, but end of lesson as it were. The lesson I've learned is, talent is really a dime-a-dozen. Everybody is talented. If talent were the discriminating factor, we would all be employed all the time. But there have to be other elements combined, infused, and associated with talent. One of them is patience. One of them is cooperation. One of them is discipline, not to be confused with obedience. Be disciplined so you can obey your director. Discipline, obedience, tenacity, and grace comprise the benchmark of the jump/how high, director/actor relationship. And I applied this in *The Full Monty*. I listened with big ears. I watched with big eyes. And I had a heart full of patience—even during those moments when I thought I knew better than the director what should happen. When I thought I knew better than the choreographer how the relationships should be orchestrated. When I thought I knew better than the composer what key the song should be in. And that's gold in the theatre.

If you were to give advice to a young actor who was having problems doing that—being patient, keeping ego out of the way, what would you say?

André De Shields: I would simply advise a young actor to listen and watch. Especially when you are in disagreement with the person or persons in charge of the creative process. You will have an opportunity to deal with a field of infinite choices once you have committed to the vision of whoever is at the helm. But if there is no commitment to the vision of the person at the helm, then your choices do not follow and there are no rewards. It isn't a favor that the director is doing for you. It really is a logical outcome of the process. By saying you are going to be part of this collaboration, you are agreeing that the director knows what's correct, what's best, what's the proper sequence or the appropriate timing. And then once that agreement is achieved, then we all share in the democratic process. But previous to that point, you have to subordinate your ego, you have to subordinate your feelings, you have to subordinate your individual needs to the benevolent totalitarianism which is the sacred terrain of the director. Of course, there are directors who will abuse that position, but they will undo themselves.

What style of communication do you most appreciate from a director?

André De Shields: I appreciate not being circumspect. I appreciate going right to the heart of the matter, because of what I just shared with you. I do not bring my feelings to the process, because I've learned I am responsible for them. If they are bruised, it isn't because my director hurt them; it's because I hurt them by bringing them to a situation where they were inappropriate. So I like a director to cut right to the chase, go right to the heart of the matter. Tell me exactly what he or she wants from me in very specific terms and I will do my best to achieve it. I'd be so bold as to say I'll guarantee hitting the target if the director sets up an absolutely unobstructed target to hit. But some directors come with all kinds of apologies and all kinds of attempts to stroke my personality which they think might be temperamental, which might be easily bruised—because those are the reputations that actors have, that we are eternally adolescent, and I suppose some of us are. But you ask me how I like it; I like it without sugarcoating.

Do you need positive reinforcement along the way?

André De Shields: Yes I do. I need positive reinforcement. I don't need therapy, but I need someone to say, "Not bad. It can be better," or "Good." I'm always suspicious of "Perfect," or "Fabulous," or "Sensational!" But I can deal with "Not bad. Good." Because there's always room for risk taking, and that's what the process is about.

An actor must be childlike with his director, he must trust, he must believe and he must not be suspicious, which is why I say when the director says, "Jump," I say "How high?" Because when you jump the net appears. If you never jump, you always wonder, "Is there a net? Is it safe? Is the pit really bottomless? Is it only dark in the abyss?" You don't know unless you jump. And when you jump, you jump on a contract of faith and trust.

Taking risks is part of the actor's work?

André De Shields: I live my life by mantras, and one of them is from French philosopher Honoré de Balzac who says, "Constant toil is the law of art as it is in life." And when you are self-absorbed you can't toil. Toil is this concept that people don't really appreciate anymore because we do everything we can not to work. But the idea of toil suggests that your work is associated with ardor.

When you work arduously, with love in your toil, that's when your art becomes spectacular. And that's when your life becomes spectacular.

Boyd Gaines

Boyd Gaines talked to us after an evening performance of *Contact*.

What insights do you have into when a director should give a note?

Boyd Gaines: I had a conversation once with Derek Jones, the director of *Wit*, who died recently. He said sometimes it would take him two or three weeks to figure out how and when to give a note. Patience is very important. Be patient and find the right time to say something. The demand for results in a neophyte director is the biggest mistake; I have to say that most inexperienced directors give notes much too soon. It is the worst thing to do. Take your time; help the actors figure out the relationships. The ideal situation is for the director to set up things in the rehearsal, to create an environment in which the play, the scenes will emerge. That is working organically. You don't have to say very much. The best thing you can do as a director, because we are all insecure, is to nurture the actors. Tom Hanks had an interviewer ask him what he looked for in a director. He said, "I want a fan." You want a director to say, "You are doing a great job, now let's fix this problem." Much of what a director does, perhaps, is fix problems. Once you develop really trusting relationships with the actors, then sometimes you have to be really hard on them. If something is blocked in the actor, then you need to find a way to get in there and fix it. The director has to be part psychologist, crafty and really patient. As a director, ask yourself, "What is my job; how can I be there to help the actors and be their ally?"

Besides guidance in fixing problems, do you need positive notes?

Boyd Gaines: I'm a person who needs a lot of positive reinforcement. If I don't get it, and if the director is someone that I like and trust well enough, I will go up to him or her and say, "You need to praise me more. Because otherwise I am spending all this time thinking that you don't like what I am doing, and I end up trying to please you, as opposed to operating under the idea that you do like me and my work and that we are going forward." Positive reinforcement always works better than negative reinforcement. Unless you run into an actor who is lazy, which is rare in the professional theatre. Sometimes you may have an actor who is difficult and you have to read them the riot act, but my experience is that most actors are really trying all the time. The problem may be that they are trying too hard. That is when a director can step in and say, "You are doing all right, just try not to work so hard." Especially in early rehearsals with an actor who is getting too far too soon. The director can gently pull them back by saying, "That is great, you can always do that, now pull it back and let's build on it." Actors want to be good and they work at it every day; if they are having trouble in a scene, they are not doing it on purpose. There are all sorts of obstacles in the way, and a really good director will always try to remove the obstacles that keep the actor from doing the work.

How do you feel about line readings?

Boyd Gaines: Directors I know really well, I allow them to give me line readings because it is faster. However, a good director will take great pains not to give one. Instead they will say, "You know I think the meaning of that line is . . ." And very often, if I trust the director I will just ask them to say it for me. Then as the actor, I can say, "Oh, I see what you're saying the meaning is." Because what you are looking for is the *thought*, the thought revealed. The last thing you want to be thinking is that the director told you to punch a certain word.

Do you like specific notes, or more general comments?

Boyd Gaines: Specificity is the thing you are always trying to nail down, and the hardest notes to receive are the general ones. The worse direction I ever got was when I was doing a long run and the director was gone, and the person maintaining the show said, "I just don't feel like you are connecting in that scene any more." And the other actor in the scene and I thought it was our best scene by far, the one where we were the most emotionally connected, the one where we were the most simple and most honest. And it was a late scene in the play, and of course the note just completely befuddled and baffled us. So we asked, "Where does it seem like we are *not* connecting?" And the response was, again, too general, "Well I couldn't really say." Generality is useless. As an actor, you just have to be unrelenting and ask for specificity, because otherwise you will throw the baby out with the bath water. And that happens sometimes. The more experienced the director, the more apt they are to be specific.

Any advice to young directors?

Boyd Gaines: I would say take voice classes; take text classes; take acting classes. The most annoying thing in the world is working with a director who has never taken an acting class. It would be like a choreographer who never took a dance class. You need a common language. The director has to know the craft when talking to actors.

Debra Monk

Debra Monk met us over lunch at a New York diner.

Can you reflect on your experiences receiving notes?

Debra Monk: As a younger actress, I always assumed if directors didn't give me notes that meant something was wrong. As I got to be more mature, I realized when most really good directors aren't saying anything, it means that you're doing it right. It took getting some positive feedback from a few directors for me to begin to trust I was doing okay when I didn't hear from them. That was one of the biggest steps I have ever taken toward knowing that I'm doing the proper work. So when a director did give me a note, I knew it was very special.

I was so panicked when I was a young actor. I was so terrified; I didn't have self-esteem. At times, my attention in a scene was about wanting people to like me. So I had to learn to overcome that. I was lucky to have a number of good directors. I was scared to go onstage and I was worried about the critics. Now I don't care. They like me or don't like me, whatever. I don't care anymore. I've changed.

What is your notion of the ideal collaboration with a director?

Debra Monk: I personally love a director who has a strong vision about what he sees, and within that vision there are 500 roads to get there. He allows me to try to find the right path, but within that, keeps me guided toward that one strong vision. I happen to be an actress who can do a scene twenty different ways. It doesn't mean I'm talented. It doesn't mean every way is good or every way is bad. I have the ability to do it. But I love to have a director who can focus me more toward this way or that one. I'll keep trying a scene many different ways; that's something that I like to do. I like to explore that way. If the director creates an environment that is safe and focused and smart, you feel like you can explore and he's going to shape it and help me. Help me look the best I can. Because I can't see what I am doing and judge if it is fulfilling the play.

To come into a play and see a director who doesn't really have a clear idea is very frustrating for actors. I work much better when directors have focus, and they have a design team that's with them. In the end, the critics may not like it. But directors who have chosen a way they believe in their heart, and they are passionate about, you can collaborate with. With a good director who I think is smart, I'll follow anything they say.

What about the nonideal situations?

Debra Monk: They are very painful. I've been in huge, million dollar musicals that are falling apart all around you. People are angry and screaming, and everybody is unhappy. In that situation you have tried-and-true Broadway people who you think would be able to handle it, but egos appear and different ideas clash and you become two different camps. "I want to do it this way." "No, I want to do it that way." And the actors are caught in between all that. Nobody is making decisions and it becomes a big mess. It's very painful, painful to go on stage.

Part of the director's job, though you may not like it, is to protect the actors from the problems going on behind the scenes, as much as possible. In small theatres, community theatres, the actors know all the stuff. It's never helpful to know all the problems that are going on. Scott Ellis is one director I've worked with who is very good about specifically handling that outside. He doesn't bring his angst to the table. Whatever is going on behind the scenes, with the producers, with the theatre or any problem he's having, you never know it. He doesn't feel the need to put that anxiety upon the actors. I've learned things after shows were over that I was shocked went on. It was very upsetting. But he handled it in the right way and through the proper channels, because it could align groups of people, splitting the company apart over it. He's very good about keeping the company focused on what they are supposed to be doing.

Any insights into knowing when it's the right time to give a note?

Debra Monk: Really good directors know they're not going to get everything the first week. They know when to wait with a note. Some of them will gently say, "What we're going toward is this." But if they ask for something too early and you're not ready to get there, you don't even know what a scene is about, it's a frustrating note. Or you're dealing with props you haven't had a chance to work with yet, and the director wants results. That is something I think directors just learn, or maybe it's an innate talent to know when to give a note, to know when to wait, and to know when to be patient. If the director is working with say, ten different actors, each one is going to have a different process. You can't always give the same note to every actor. It's not going to work. Some actors need a lot more attention than others do. Some need to carry their scripts almost to the end. Others get off the script right away. I guess really good directors are able to handle all those many, many actors. I worked with Mark Brokaw. He was a wonderful director, a young director. I was so impressed. He would take so many notes, but he didn't give them all. He took them all because he had to get them all down. And I asked him, "How did you know at such a young age that you don't have to give all those notes?" He had the ability to tell who needed help right away and who needed more time to try something.

Some directors get impatient; maybe young directors want to get every problem solved immediately. But there's a way to do it and keep the actors reassured. Say, "This has been a difficult day, don't worry about it, we'll spend a lot of time on this, you don't have to worry," or "We're going to take the scene bit by bit, because there's twenty people on stage, with all this stuff." And you think, "Great! It's taken care of." Rather than, "Oh my God. Where do I go? What do I do?" I always find that more helpful.

It's knowing how to stay calm and communicate?

Debra Monk: Yes. Some directors can do that, others can't. If an actor is totally going the wrong direction, I think a lot of directors cannot do it gently. I've never thought that anger, or putting anybody down or making them feeling less than others is any way to work with an actor. But I know some directors do that because they have to get a performance out of the actor. I just don't believe that you have to bully people or make them feel bad about themselves. I don't think it works.

Linda Purl

Linda Purl answered some questions during a break in the technical rehearsals for *Tom Sawyer*.

What qualities do you look for in a director?

Linda Purl: A director who is prepared, one who knows the script backwards and forwards and has studied it through the lens of each character. When you are allowed to discover something about your character for yourself, then you tend to own it. Therefore, I prefer a director who has his own answer to every question but does not rush to give you that information. I remember working with a director who did not give us blocking. In one instance he said, "Why don't you start with this pile of books, and maybe by the end of the scene, get the pile of books moved over to the shelf, if you want." We tried it a few times, and just getting that little bit of a sense of where he wanted me to be was very helpful. Now I assumed he had not blocked the play. I assumed he had given me all the information he had in his mind. And one day, I was standing next to him to ask him a question, and I glanced down at his script which was turned to a page we had yet to block, and it was fully diagrammed. Completely blocked in his mind. He was secure enough not to have to impose all of that on us, but to give us just a little hint of what he wanted. So we really had the best of both worlds. We had someone who was in control, who was also secure enough to allow us our own discovery process.

I love a director who is able to create a positive, nonjudgmental atmosphere, because what that gives you in the rehearsal room is the permission to fail. The permission to be utterly foolish. And it's through failing, oftentimes, that you find what is right, true, what is possible.

If you enjoy discovering things on your own, how do you feel about directors giving you specific notes?

Linda Purl: I don't mind being given very specific notes, though I know some actors who really have a bad reaction to it. What I can't use, what is of no value to me, is a director who says, "Don't play the scene angry. Don't do something." Because you can't stand there and *not* do something. You have to *do* something. It's like someone telling you, "Now don't think about the elephant." It's a useless statement.

How do you like a director to communicate to you?

Linda Purl: Encouragement is always welcome, but I find it destructive for a director to say, "That was perfect," or "Do it exactly that way again." You can't. When you get to that moment it's invariably all you are thinking about, like a neon sign in your brain, and you'll never find "perfection" again. It's simply not helpful.

I worked with a fantastic director once; we were all having a drink after rehearsal and he was talking with one of the actresses. She got up and left and the director said, "I haven't found the key to her yet." Which was a revelation to me because his gift as a director was to find specifically what worked for that person. To find some way into that person's art. Something quirky in their sense of humor. Some interest, so then he could speak to them in the metaphor that would work for them. For instance, a director said to me once, "It's like when you're running from the cop down at the end of the block." But I've never run from a cop around the corner; I didn't have a childhood in which these things happened. Although the image had great power for him, it had no resonance for me. The former director I mentioned had a real gift for being intuitive about a particular actor and, therefore, could be specific with his notes.

Any tips on dealing with your ego during disagreements and frustrations?

Linda Purl: Breathe.

Try to get a perspective for the moment, and then get a real perspective in terms of your life. And then oftentimes when you come back to it, things will be calmer; things shift a little bit. And make sure it's not personal. Make sure that it's really just about the work, that it's not based on your like or dislike of a particular trait in someone or yourself. Go back to the script. That's your bible; it won't fail you. It helps you in the discipline of getting yourself out of the way.

How do you keep a performance fresh night after night, especially after a good night when you feel pressured to recreate what you did?

Linda Purl: The only thing I've found that works is to mentally go deeper into the text, into the specific circumstance of your character. Also, and this is hard to do, but don't judge yourself. I worked once with some senior actors in a very, very wordy play and on occasion they would lose their way—anybody would have really. Not so the audience would have known, but you knew; they knew. Both of them did an unusual thing, which was that they would find their way back to the correct dialogue and not judge themselves for a moment. They just picked themselves up and immediately jumped off the cliff again. They were fearless. I think my natural inclination would be to freeze up emotionally and just concentrate on the words. Of course then there's no room for any inspiration to flow. These actors had the discipline of not judging themselves. It sounds simple, but the only people I've seen do it really well were actors in their 70s.

Karen Ziemba

Karen Ziemba sat for an interview before her matinee performance of *Contact*.

What kind of director do you like to work with?

Karen Ziemba: I like a director to have ideas, but before the actual rehearsal process begins, it's imperative that they have a theme, or a very clear idea of what story we are all going to tell. That, of course, begins with the director's creative team who creates a visual and audible world for the character(s) to inhabit; then they bring that vision to the first day of rehearsal, so the actors can begin to bring that vision to life. Rehearsal can be an incredibly fruitful and collaborative time, sometimes an actor's favorite part of doing a show. When a director is a true collaborator with all of his company, respects their suggestions and yet, can divulge his or her own specific ideas with conviction and clarity, you're in for a pretty smooth sail. Personally, if a director also is very inspirational as a human being and shares their passion for the show they're working on with their company in all aspects of the rehearsal and performance process, whether you're sharing a huge laugh or arguing a point till you're at your wits end, that turns me on!

What happens when a director gives you an idea you don't agree with?

Karen Ziemba: It is important to listen to your director, but also have the ability to say to yourself, "You know what? I don't know if that's ever going to work for me, but I'm going to try it because they've asked me to." It's having reverence for a director and what they have to impart. I have to start in the position of feeling as if the director has something to divulge that is going to *help* my performance. I've been very fortunate, because that has been the case most of the time. Hopefully, an idea or a direction makes sense for both of you.

What can a director do to be the kind of director you revere?

Karen Ziemba: I don't think directors always have to be sweetness and light. "Hey, how you doing?" You know, your best bud; it's not about that. But, I think it's important for the director to be the one in control. I like it when the actors do not cow a director, because when an actor is in charge of rehearsal, everything becomes about him. And I would prefer it if it was the director running the rehearsal and we have the director's ideas. Sometimes it happens that an actor's view of the play is more "on the money," more succinct or thought out than the director's, and when that happens, I think you're in a difficult position. Because I don't feel a director should be somebody who just moves chairs around and tells you where to walk. A director should be more prepared and have more to offer than that. They must leap all the way in and be willing to make mistakes. Not come in as a know-it-all, but as a collaborator: open-minded, with specific ideas, and yet open enough to learn from the actors too.

Directors have to wear so many hats and have so many things to think about. They have to be intelligent, resilient, and have good people skills, whether it is the skill to tell somebody off in the right way or the skill to make somebody feel better when they're down or needy. They have to be part therapist, part ringleader, and part opening comic who sets the tone. It starts from the top and there's a trickle-down effect. It's advantageous if they are strong, in control, and approachable.

What kind of notes do you like to receive?

Karen Ziemba: You know what I've always liked, and some people may think this is a bit sophomoric, but I like 3 × 5 cards. I like it when the assistants to the director or the directors themselves jot down notes on cards. So when you get your notes, it's not only discussed but they have been handed to you. So you can either chuck them in the trash or you can hold onto them and think them over. There's something about having that tangible writing, as opposed to getting a quick comment, on the fly. Especially in summer stock situations where you only have notes for one or two days at most. I'm sure some actors might be offended by getting little 3 × 5 cards, but I like it. I want those reminders right there with me, because there's too many other things to think about.

Do you want notes to be phrased in a positive, complimentary way?

Karen Ziemba: Susan Stroman does this all the time. Other directors too. They'll say, "That note I gave you—you nailed it, it's great—*but*, there's this one section that always is such and such." They start out with an encouraging remark, or something positive, and then continue on with the stuff that needs to be worked on. They don't come in berating and punching, so you have to come in with your dukes up. That is the worst treatment I think, especially when you're dealing with adults.

I did *Jerome Robbins' Broadway*, speaking of reverence; his work is so amazing. When I was in the middle of performing it, I felt so wonderful; it was such incredible work. But the way he treated people, it was humiliating. You'd hold back tears, you wanted to scream at him, "How could you say that!" He would call you stupid, he would scream at you, he wouldn't call you by your first name. He had this berating way of directing, bullying you into it, scaring you.

He'd say, "Put her understudy on!" He'd do stuff like that. You'd be speechless. That was the way he got results. That was *his* way. It worked for him. He didn't mind not being liked.

How do you feel about receiving notes after a show has opened?

Karen Ziemba: It's good for me. If somebody comes back the next night and is still pounding you, pounding you, pounding you, that's one thing. But if they come back after a month or two and they remind you of something, it really helps. Sometimes what happens in live performance is, you start getting too broad, doing more than you need to do, making "improvements." And a reminder of little things like that can pull you in the right direction. And the fact that someone's even interested in coming back is great.

Glossary

Action: the tactics the character uses to achieve his/her objective.

Active Verb: a verb in its infinitive tense, used to label an action.

Anticipating the Moment: reacting to or preparing to react to something before it has happened on stage, see also Telegraphing.

Arc: the forward momentum of the action or story, as structured through a clear beginning, middle, and end (of a play, scene, or unit of a scene).

Beat: a unit of action in a play script, usually delineated by a change in tactics, a change in subject matter, a shift of focus from one dominant character to another or an entrance or exit of a character.

Exposition: when action that has occurred prior to the play or scene is revealed.

Given Circumstances: the facts of the play script including geographical location, date, time of day, season, and year; economic, political, social, and religious environments; previous action and character background.

Inner Monologue: the unspoken thoughts of the character.

Intention: what the character wants (desires) in a scene; the Objective.

Moment Before: what has happened to a character just prior to making an entrance.

Objective: see Intention.

Obstacle: what is in the way of the character achieving his/her objective, often another person.

Overall Objective: what the character wants in the play, also called the Super Objective.

Physical Scoring: breaking down the movement of the character.

Plot: what happens to the characters in the play; see also Story.

Scoring: breaking down the text into units of action.

Stichomythia: a quick sequence of short lines between two or more characters.

Story: how the action unfolds.

Subtext: the underlying meaning of the line; what is implied by the line.

Super Objective: see Overall Objective.

Telegraphing: indicating to the audience what is coming next, either physically or vocally.

Unit of Action: division of the script into smaller sections of action; see also Beat.

Willing Suspension of Disbelief: the audience agreeing to believe that for the duration of the play what is happening on stage is real.

World of the Play: date, time, era, and given circumstances of the play as set out by the playwright and conceptualized by the director and designers.